BELIEVE IT OR NOT———

Believe it or not!

A Modern Book of Wonders, Miracles, Freaks, Monstrosities and almost-Impossibilities, Written, Illustrated and Proved by Robert L. Ripley, or

PUBLISHING

Copyright ©2004 by Ripley Entertainment Inc.
All rights reserved. Ripley's, Believe It or Not!, and Ripley's Believe It or Not!
are registered trademarks of Ripley Entertainment Inc.

No part of this publication may be reproduced in whole or in part, or stored in a
retrieval system, or transmitted in any form or by any means, electronic, mechanical,
photocopying, recording, or otherwise, without written permission from the publisher.
For information regarding permission, write to VP Intellectual Property, Ripley
Entertainment Inc., Suite 188, 7576 Kingspointe Parkway, Orlando, Florida 32819

Library of Congress Control Number: 2004096481

ISBN 1-893951-09-X

This special reprint of the original edition published in 1929 celebrates
75 years of Ripley publishing.

Printed in the United States of America
in March / 2011 by Berryville Graphics
2nd Printing

BELIEVE IT OR NOT

PREFACE

I MAKE a living out of the fact that truth is stranger than fiction. The "Believe It or Not" pictures that appear in a hundred or so newspapers throughout the country are drawn according to that scale.

Yet, I venture to say that I have been called a liar more often than anybody in the world. Ordinarily when one is called a liar—well, to say the least, one feels hurt. (Sometimes it follows that somebody gets hurt.) But it is different with me. I do not mind it a bit. When I am called a liar by a reader of my cartoons I feel flattered! That short and ugly word is like music to my ears. I am complimented, because it means to me that my cartoon that day contained some strange fact that was unbelievable—and therefore most interesting, and that the reader did not know the truth when he saw it. That is the time when I always think of the comment made by Hamlet on a certain occasion:

> "There are more things in heaven and earth, Horatio,
> Than are dreamt of in your philosophy."

I shall not forget the day my cartoon appeared with the illustrated statement that "Lindbergh was the sixty-seventh man to make a non-stop flight over the Atlantic Ocean." Who would believe a statement like that? Three thousand wrote in to tell me that they did not. It is true, however. Who will believe that "a day is forty-eight hours long—not twenty-four"; "that Methuselah died before his father"; that "Buffalo Bill never shot a buffalo in his life"; that "a man died of old age before he was seven years old." Can anybody be expected to believe that "a river runs backward"; "a flower eats mice"; "Napoleon crossed the Red Sea—as Moses did—on dry land"; "Fish climb trees," etc.?

Those who "doubt truth to be a liar" may be forgiven. The mail brings about a thousand letters a week from readers hoping to catch me in error. Which they never do. (Well, hardly ever.)

Sometimes a reader is blinded by the shining countenance of truth and stumbles into error. Not long ago I printed a short sentence in one of my pictures that contained all the letters of the alphabet. This is it:

John P. Brady gave me a black walnut box of quite a small size.

The next morning brought thirteen letters pointing out that I had left the letter "F" out of the sentence. Now, there was no mistake on my part—all the letters of the alphabet, including the letter "F" were in that sentence, but what a strange thing it was that thirteen readers failed to find it and that each of them thought the same letter was missing.

i.

The first "Believe It or Not" cartoon was an accident.

I had been drawing cartoons for the sports pages for some time when, in the course of a day's work, I hurriedly put together a few athletic oddities that happened to be lying on my desk and made them up into a cartoon— never for a moment expecting that it meant any more than a day's work done . . . and for the want of a better caption I called it "Believe It or Not."

It appeared the next day in the old New York Globe, and much to my surprise there was considerable comment about it. The editor of the paper suggested that I make another one if I "could gather together enough stunts." A week later I had enough facts for another one, and it seemed to be more popular than my usual run of cartoons. Thereafter I made a "Believe It or Not" cartoon a week. A year later, I made two a week, and soon the demand came that I make one every day. Now it looks as though I will never do anything else. And I don't care if I do.

I would like to answer the common question:

"Where do you get all the strange things that you draw about?"

Everywhere, all the time.

Here and there—day and night; through observation, conversation, and edification. I am constantly searching—everywhere all the time.

Travel, of course, is an unfailing source of oddities—"The world's mine oyster." Once or twice each year I venture forth to foreign lands for pearls to string in the "Believe It or Not" columns of the newspapers. I have traveled in sixty-four different countries, and hope to see them all before I am through. (Oh, yes, there are more than sixty-four countries.)

Sometimes suggestions are sent in to me, but, unfortunately, the usable ones are rare. Someday I hope to meet James Waldo Fawcett, of New York, Doc Applegate, of Ogallala, Neb., and J. Dennis Butler, of Alameda, Cal., and thank them for their interesting contributions. They are among the few who know what is interesting to people other than themselves.

I have been drawing the "Believe It or Not" pictures for eight years and find that it grows easier each day. There is no danger of running out of material (as some readers think): the supply is inexhaustible.

> "This world is all a fleeting show,
> For man's illusion given."

I have enough "queeriosities" on hand to make a hundred cartoons, and a library of strange facts and curious bits of knowledge enough to fill several books like this one. (A fair warning!)

ii.

CONTENTS

CONTENTS—*Continued*

CONTENTS—*Continued*

CONTENTS—*Continued*

CONTENTS—*Continued*

CONTENTS—*Continued*

FULL PAGE ILLUSTRATIONS

BELIEVE IT OR NOT———

AN ODYSSEY OF ODDITIES

≈❧≈

TO OBTAIN material, and to gather strange facts and to portray queer people that go to make up the daily "Believe It or Not" pictures it has been necessary for me to get about the world a bit.

"Seeing Is Believing"

I have traveled in 64 countries—including Hell (Norway), and the strangest thing I saw was man. Man may be the noblest work of God—but even the good Lord must have his joke sometimes. The world was made in seven days, and man in a perpetual daze. The Lord placed a funny-looking little fellow on the earth without telling him what it was all about or where he came from or where he was going. This funny-looking little chap has been running about trying to find out ever since.

"Strange Is Man When He Seeks After His Gods."

Therefore the strangest places on earth are the holiest. And the strangest and most remarkable city in the world is the holy city of Benares on the muddy arm of the Ganges, India's holy river. Here amidst a crumbling confusion of holy places is a temple—The Nepalese Temple. About fifteen feet up on the outside is a frieze of sculptured figures representing in succession the eighty-one sinful positions.

Sin is the curse of the human race—although it is very popular. The question of what causes sin has perplexed the ages. But of all the doctrines which men have propounded in their endeavors to solve the permanent enigma of existence, probably none has had a more potent influence than that which holds that the spirit is eternally pure and that all matter is inherently bad. The spirit of man is pure but his flesh is wicked, and therefore should be subjected to various degrees of mortification.

This gives rise to the various penances and punishments and ascetic practices so highly honored in all great religions.

1

The 81 sinful positions around the Nepalese Temple are counter-balanced by the same number of positions of punishment. These positions of penitence are practiced by an army of ascetics throughout India—particularly in the holy cities of Benares, Allahabad, Lahore, Mysore, and Calcutta. These sects of ascetics are probably the strangest men of mankind. They are sometimes called Faquirs (often they are fakers), Sadhus, Yogis, etc.

They presume to renounce the world and its ways, cast off their clothing and cover their naked bodies with ashes which gives them a weird white appearance; they neither cut nor comb their hair and usually plaster their heads with cow-dung (as evidence that the cow is holy in India) and adopt one of the ingenious methods of self-torture with the idea of keeping themselves constantly conscious of their penance. They are most often found about the holy places and always flock to all the religious festivals in the sacred cities along the Ganges where they are frequently made objects of veneration by the muddled multitudes of India who shower them with food and money. I have never heard one of them ask for alms, and they accept all offerings in stony silence.

THE GHATS OF THE GANGES

AS I stood on the steps of Dasashwamedh—steps worn smooth by countless thousands of pious ones descending into the water—the sight before my eyes impressed me more than any other in the world.

Nowhere on earth can you see such a weird cross-cut of human life with all of its spiritual and social manifestations set in such a background of picturesque architecture as along the crescent-shaped shore of the holy Ganges.

Several miles to either side extend the bathing ghats, wide flights of stately steps sinking down into the sacred waters. Surmounting them are the strange towers and temples of their gods and the palaces and places of their kings. Above and in back are the narrow streets and lanes which connect the ghats with one another—a bewildering mass of mouldering alleyways, too narrow for wheeled traffic, and overhung by crumbling buildings that reminded me of Canton. These are the "Pukka Mahals." And so this is Benares!

Crowding my way down the steps of the ghat, among the weirdest collection of humanity on the face of the earth—demented, deluded, diseased, and devout—all struggling after their gods, I clambered aboard a boat and floated slowly down the Ganges before all this pagan panorama, wonder-

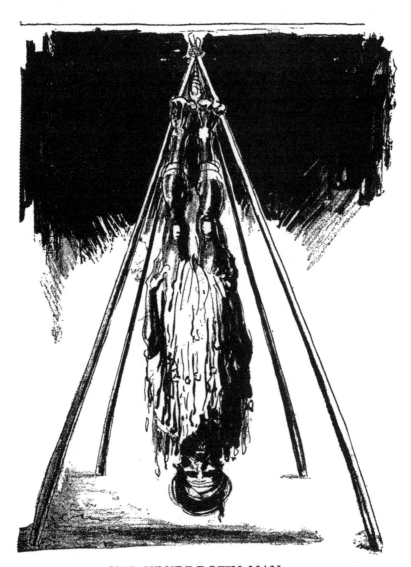

THE UPSIDE-DOWN MAN

The Urdhamukhi Sadhu who hangs head downward for three hours at a time.

ing all the while whether leprosy were contagious, and whether that one-eyed beggar with spots and both hands and feet eaten away had tainted me with that unmerciful malady with the red stump of his hand when he nudged me as I passed.

Each ghat and each temple is different. Each is built and dedicated to a different deity and each spot is peculiarly holy to a Hindoo—from the Assi Ghat, built at the junction of a river not visible to anybody but the Hindoo, down past several hundred ghats to the Prahlad Ghat, the last of all.

Five of these ghats are particularly holy, and the millions of pilgrims must immerse in each successively on the same day—the Assi, Dasashwamedh, Barna-sangam, Panchganga, and the Manikarnika. Some are built in honor of monkeys, others, to "Ganesh," a red idol with three eyes, a silver cap, and an elephant's trunk, riding on a rat. Another was built for the "Dandas," ascetics who always carry long sticks upright, never putting them down. The Sitla Ghat was built in honor of "Mother Smallpox," and the Dasashwamedh Ghat means the "ghat of the ten-horse sacrifice."

All the ghats are thronged with multitudes who swarm down in multi-colored waves to the filthy—but purifying—water.

Strange, but it seems that the dirtier a thing is the holier it becomes in India!

Sanitation and sanctity never come together here. The holy water of the Ganges is muddy and sluggish. Into it empty the city sewers and into it are thrown the dead who are too poor to afford the wood with which to burn their bodies after death. Those who die of loathsome diseases such as small-pox and leprosy are regarded as unworthy of cremation and so are consigned also to the great river.

According to their creed, the holy Ganges water purifies everything, utterly and instantly. Nothing can defile it, no matter how foul.

So the sight of these throngs of people drinking and bathing in this filthy water in which dead bodies are floating and sewage is seeping is not to be wondered at—but you will shudder at it just the same.

I was rowed up and down this panorama of never-ceasing interest all morning and I wish space permitted me to tell all I saw. I had the boat stop near the tall, stately minarets of the Aurangzeb Mosque near where thin columns of smoke were slowly ascending. Climbing over several native boats I reached the shore where several gauze-draped corpses were resting with their feet in the water.

Just above me were several bodies burning.

THE BURNING GHAT

I HAD seen burning ghats before and was not particularly anxious to see this one at the Jalsain Ghat. However, when I learned that more than a million human beings offered up a daily prayer that they be burned on this very spot I decided to watch the entire ceremony.

I have seen many dead people in India—it is a common thing to die here—and frequently I have seen the bodies being wrapped in winding sheets of thin gauze as they lay on the ground in front of a hut. When a death occurs the body is immediately taken out of the house. If it is that of a woman it is wrapped in red; if it is that of a man it is covered over with white. Children are not wrapped at all, and neither are those who die of leprosy or smallpox. They are simply taken down to the Ganges and thrown in.

This morning on my way to the Burning Ghat I saw two funerals on the way. The procession is simple. There is no hearse—the body is merely tied to a bamboo pole by the neck and ankles and hoisted on the shoulders of two chanting relatives, who carry it down to the river bank.

I arrived at the Burning Ghat before them, passing the Nepalese Temple with its eighty-one indecent carvings, and the Dharm Kup, the sacred well in which the lepers bathe and where the water is changed but once a year. I stood for a few minutes watching the ghastly fires of several corpses leaping viciously to the sky, when behind me came the chanting of the procession I had passed near the Chowk.

Down the crumbling steps they went to the edge of the sacred water and advancing gave the body its last bath in the holy Ganges, for without that bath any shadow which might fall upon it would convey impurity. Then, resting the feet of the white-robed figures in the water, the two bearers set about building the funeral pyre.

An ordinary pile of logs and boughs, about four feet high, costs five dollars. This was just an ordinary one. The body was placed on top and several cakes of cow dung laid on its chest, while the nearest relative, the dead man's wife, ascended a few steps to a sacred spot where the holy fire was brought to burn the body.

As I waited a sacred cow came wandering down the steps and calmly proceeded to eat the grass strands that bound the winding sheet to the corpse. The widow returned with shaven head and snow-white garments, waited for the cow to finish, then placed a handful of meal on her dead husband's mouth, walked five times around the pyre and without the slightest sign of emotion set fire to the pile at her husband's throat.

The flames spread rapidly. From time to time the woman, assisted by a near relative, used long poles to make the fire burn faster. Not a pleasant sight.

You are never so dead as when you die in India.

When the fire died away the widow threw the remaining parts into the Ganges. The relatives led her to the water's edge and broke the jewelry from her wrists and ankles and threw them into the water also. Then, filling an earthen jar with the sacred water, she placed it on her shoulder, ascended to the smouldering pyre, and tipped it backward from her shoulder onto the glowing ashes of her master. Straightway she walked on up the steps; never again will she look backward at the spot.

On and up she went through an archway where monkeys were clambering and above which several vultures were soaring. And just as she disappeared from sight into the dingy crevices—called streets—of the Pukka Mahals she passed by a high platform on top of which is an image of Mahadeva where the worshippers of Mahadeva dwell, a sect supposedly immune to the possibility of earthly defilement.

So they say.

from life
— Benares, India.

THE SUN GAZER

"STRANGE is man when he seeks after his gods." Sometimes he thinks too much and seeks too long, yet learns nothing and loses everything . . . like the naked faquir who sits all day glaring at the blazing sun. He has looked too long and now sees nothing. The fiery rays of the sun have burned out his eyes long years ago.

Each morning as I floated down the sacred stream I saw this sun gazer being carried down the steps to his accustomed place on the Dasashwamedh Ghat. His brothers placed him down gently—he could not walk as his legs had withered away from years of inactivity—and turned his face toward the east. Slowly he opened his eyes to greet the morning sun as it raised its burning head over the temple tops of the Holy City; here he remained the whole day long with his wide staring eyes fastened on the blazing sun without once turning them away or closing them for an instant until the dying disc had sunk once more below the horizon. He had been doing this for fifteen years.

BURIED ALIVE

"SAMADAI," the act of suspended animation, is a power long claimed by the Hindus. Although I was not fortunate enough to witness a performance of this seeming impossibility, there are many reliable records of such burials and subsequent restorations.

The best known performance of this mysterious power of suspending the functions of the body (with the exception of a faint heart action) was given before the Maharajah Runjeet Singh in Lahore during the summer of 1837. A Yogi by the name of Haridas attained "samadai" and was buried in the ground for forty days, after which he was dug up again and revived. Yogi Haridas fell into a trance and his assistants stopped his nose, mouth, ears, and eyes with wax; then, wrapping him in a winding cloth, they lowered him into a grave and filled it tight with earth. A guard was placed about the spot to prevent trickery. When the Yogi was uncovered forty days later he appeared slightly emaciated but otherwise was little the worse for his remarkable experience.

8

Yogi Haridas, by the way, was the same Yogi who could touch his forehead with his tongue. (See page 35.)

The various "Rama Beys" etc., who have been appearing in American vaudeville recently with "buried alive" acts in which they claim the power to suspend animation are merely tricksters. None of them ever saw India—as a matter of fact, the most successful one is an Italian. Houdini performed the same trick under water.

Hindoos are credited with marvelous powers of magic, but I was unable to see any of it. They do remarkable sleight-of-hand work, and I had a faquir do the tree-growing trick on my bed-room floor. It is a fair trick, but in my opinion, Thurston and Houdini were far more clever than any Hindoo.

THE BED OF NAILS

SADHUS who sit on beds of sharp spikes have been more or less featured in the Sunday supplements of our country. This stunt is a popular one in India and I saw half a dozen of them. In Mysore a six-year-old boy was starting out in life by assuming a sitting position on a home-made "kiddie car" of nails.

One old fellow that I saw in Benares had been on his trundle bed for eighteen years, I was told. After some persuasion, highly emphasized with rupees, the venerable old faquir stood up on his spiny mattress and gave me the opportunity to see that there was no fake about it.

THE EVER-STANDING MEN

THEY were standing by the river not far from the Kali-Ghat in Calicut. They had been standing for ten years or more without once sitting down, and were apparently prepared to remain upright the rest of their lives. I doubt if there be two more homely objects. Their bodies and faces were smeared a dirty sickly white leaving two black spots for their eyes which were divided by perpendicular red and yellow caste marks. They had forced two poles into the sand from which were suspended arm rests on which they leaned now and then, but never at any time did they take their weight entirely off their feet, or attempt to sit down in any manner.

HUMAN INCH-WORMS

PILGRIMAGES are quite the thing in the Far East. All Mohammedans hope to make a pilgrimage to Mecca before they die. All Hindoos hope to bathe at least once in the Ganges at Benares. Their penchant for penitence has created some ingenious methods of locomotion. They come crawling and rolling long distances to their temples on the Ganges. One deluded disciple of Siva crawled all the way from the Himalayas taking more than two years to make the journey.

I happened to be in the Kali-Ghat Temple one day and witnessed the finish of one of these pilgrimages of penance. A woman—followed by a curious crowd—was progressing by means of a series of prostrations. Standing up straight she would extend her arms above her head and then kneel and slide her hands forward on the ground until she was lying at full length on her face in the dust. Keeping her finger tips to the ground she raised the rest of her body in much the same way as an inch-worm and gaining her feet she stepped along until her toes reached the tips of her fingers—then she stood up again and repeated the performance. She had been traveling many days in this fashion to reach the Kali-Ghat. The Goddess Kali, the object of her struggles, is a large black figure with four arms, three red eyes, a long scarlet tongue reaching out three feet from the mouth, a necklace of human skulls, and no legs.

The curse of India is the Hindoo religion. More than two hundred million people believe a motley mixture of mythology that is strangling the nation.

"He who yearns for God in India soon loses his head as well as his heart."

Modern Hindoo theology is a development of several ancient and odd forms of worship, the first form of which was called Vedism—the worship of

AN EVER-STANDING MAN

A HINDU URDHABAHU HELD HIS ARMS ABOVE HIS HEAD FOR 20 YEARS!

nature. Some, representing these sects of the middle ages, still survive and we see them about the streets of Calcutta, particularly at the Kali-Ghat Temple: Nail-men, whose nails grow until they pierce their palms; Sky-facers, who hold their faces rigidly upward till unable to bend them back; Up-arm men, who hold up their arms in the same way until they wither away; Tree-men, who hang upside down in trees like monkeys; Skull-men and Pot-men, who carry these symbols, and other forms of religious fanatics.

Most of the wretches that we see around the holy places of worship have no idea what their attitudes and symbols mean; all are intellectually degraded and some are mere fakers.

The modern Hindoo has one God who pervades everything, called Brahma. His three personal manifestations are as Brahma, the Creator; Vishnu, the Preserver; and Siva, the Destroyer. Brahma is generally represented with four heads and four arms, in which he holds various symbolical objects. From Brahma, Vishnu, and Siva have sprung a multitude of lesser gods, whom the Hindoos, faithful to their practice of exaggeration, reckon up to the astounding total of 330,000,000.

The Hindoos believe that all evil proceeds from antecedent evil and that the penalty must be suffered in each succeeding existence. There are eighty-four lakhs (8,400,000) of different species of animals through which the soul of man is liable to pass, and the Hindoo's object is to rid himself of this series of continuous transmigrations so that he may live in the same heaven with his god.

To this end he makes offerings to the image of a god, abstains from killing any animal, gives money to priests; does penance which at times extends to severe bodily torture, propitiates demons and keeps strictly the rules of caste. And there are almost a hundred different castes, each entirely separate with regard to marriage and trades.

This, briefly, is Hindooism.

Sounds almost unbelievable, doesn't it? Yet more than twice as many people as there are in all the United States believe such things with a burning fervor that we, as Christians, cannot understand.

A strange country is India!

13

A POUND OF FEATHERS WEIGHS MORE THAN A POUND OF GOLD

A pound is a pound you say?

Not always.

A pound of feathers weighs more than a pound of gold because feathers are weighed by "avoirdupois" weight which has 16 ounces to a pound, while gold is always weighed by "troy" weight which only contains 12 ounces to a pound.

A GALLON OF VINEGAR WEIGHS MORE IN THE WINTER THAN IN THE SUMMER

This is puzzling—but a fact nevertheless.

The difference in weight is due entirely to the contraction and expansion of the vinegar due to the changes in temperature. During the heat of the summer months the vinegar, as any other liquid, will expand and thus the weight will be slightly less because a gallon jug will hold less.

A gallon jug of 4 per cent. (Acetic Acid) cider vinegar measured at 80 degrees (Farenheit) or summer heat, weighed 8.403 pounds—or 134½ ounces. When the same gallon jug filled with the same vinegar was measured at 40 degrees (Farenheit), or winter temperature, it weighed 8.457 pounds—or 135½ ounces. In other words, a gallon of vinegar will weigh approximately one ounce more in the winter than in the summer.

THE BOY WHO DIED OF OLD AGE BEFORE
HE WAS SEVEN YEARS OLD

THIS strange anomaly of an aged youth attracted considerable attention during the last century. He was Charles Charlesworth, born of normal parents in Staffordshire, England, March 14, 1829. He reached maturity and grew whiskers at the age of four and died suddenly in a faint (syncope) when but seven years old.

Charlesworth was of small stature and proportions, and with imperfectly developed clavicles, lower jaw, and membrane bones of the skull. His face was wizened, hair and whiskers white, skin shriveled, hands knotted with conspicuous veins and tendons, voice piping, and gait and standing posture those of an old man.

Ref.: "Progeria" and "Premature Senility" in any Medical Text Book.

THE LONGEST FIGHT

THE longest battle within the ropes of a squared circle took place in the Olympic Club of New Orleans, April 6, 1893, between Andy Bowen (colored) and Jack Burke.

The contest lasted 110 rounds—7 hours, 19 minutes.

Iron men! Doubtless that will be your comment; but the irony of it all was the fact that the referee, Jack Duffy, stopped the struggle in the 110th round and declared it "no-contest."

Following is the report as it appeared in the Police Gazette on the day following the match:

THE LONG-WINDED BOWEN-BURKE FIGHT AT NEW ORLEANS

The Bowen-Burke fight took place last Thursday night and Friday morning before several thousand spectators at the Olympic Club in New Orleans. It was stopped Friday morning in the 110th round by the referee, Jack Duffy, who decided that it was no contest. The purse will probably be divided. Bowen wanted to fight to a finish. The bones in both of Burke's hands were broken.

Bowen, who is a New Orleans man, and Burke, a Texan, fought for a $2,500 purse, of which the loser was to get $500, and the light-weight championship of the South. The betting previous to the fight favored New Orleans, and the largest crowd ever held by the Olympic Clubhouse was in attendance when the men en-tered the ring. That was at 9.30 o'clock Thursday night. In the twenty-fifth round Bowen was near-ly knocked down and out by two punches on the head. His opponent failed to follow up his advantage.

Burke got a stiff punching in the twenty-eighth, and from then on up to the forty-fifth round the contest was dull and uninteresting. At the end of the forty-eighth Burke was knocked down and was only saved by the call of time for the interval between rounds. The crowd whistled "Home, Sweet Home," and at midnight many hundreds deserted the clubhouse for home. It was one of the poorest fights that had ever taken place in New Orleans, although both men were in perfect condition.

* * *

THE MAN WHO WAS "SEEN TO DEATH"

WEI CHIEH, son of Wei Huan (286-312), was popularly known as "The Jewel" on account of his great beauty. At the age of five his handsome face and graceful form caused the populace to regard him as a supernatural being.

He joined the establishment of the Heir-Apparent of China, but during political troubles it was necessary for him to flee to the city of Nanking where he was exposed to the populace who crowded around him in such numbers and stared so hard that he was actually "seen to death."

HENRY LEWIS
PLAYING BILLIARDS WITH HIS NOSE
MADE A RUN OF 46

17

THE CLOCK OF HEAVEN

IF the stars in the northern sky are visible, says *Popular Mechanics*, you can set your watch by them within fifteen minutes of the correct time and without the use of a complicated table. The polestar is considered as the center of a huge clock and the pointer of the Dipper, the hour hand. The numeral six will be below the polestar and twelve above. Taking the time as indicated by the Dipper's pointers, you can add to that figure the number of months that have elapsed since the first of January to the nearest quarter month. The resulting sum is doubled and subtracted from sixteen and a quarter. If the result is more than sixteen and a quarter, subtract it from forty and a quarter. The answer is time in hours after noon. For instance, it is late September and the pointers of the sky clock correspond to the position of the hour hand at seven o'clock. Eight and three-fourths months have elapsed since New Year's Day. This is added to seven, making fifteen and three-quarters. Double this is thirty-one and one-half. Subtracting from forty and one-quarter gives eight and three-quarters, or 8:45 P. M.

* * *

PUNISHMENT BY PROXY

IN GERMANY during the nineteenth century all Princes of the blood had their "Prügelknaben"—that is, a boy who was brought up with the young Prince and who was spanked every time the Prince misbehaved.

* * *

MAKING WHOOPEE!

LORD EDWARD RUSSELL was host at a party where 6,000 men got drunk. A fountain was used as a punch bowl into which 25 hogsheads of brandy were poured, and among the other ingredients used were 25,000 lemons and 1,300 pounds of sugar. London, Oct. 25, 1799.

* * *

THE KING'S ENGLISH

King George I, of England, could not speak one word of English.

* * *

BYE! BYE! BLACK SHEEP

During a storm in Lapleau, France, lightning struck into a sheep fold, killing every black sheep but leaving all the white sheep unharmed.

* * *

WHAT'S IN A NAME

All female rulers named Jane were murdered, became insane, or were deposed.

A FOOTBALL GAME (Rugby).
WAS PLAYED BY MATANI SAVAGES
OF WEST AFRICA —
USING A HUMAN SKULL
FOR A BALL

A CAT
ADOPTED AND
MOTHERED
A RAT

Owned by FRANCES PITT — England 1916.

A PUMPKIN — WEIGHING 100 POUNDS
— AND MEASURING 6½ FEET IN CIRCUMFERENCE
WAS RAISED BY AL. CLAYBERG, of Mt. Kisco, N.Y. 1924

FRANK
BROWN
wounded soldier
CAN SMOKE A
CIGARETTE
THRU A HOLE IN
HIS FOREHEAD

19

ALL THE NAMES OF GOD HAVE FOUR LETTERS

LORD	English.
JHVH	(JeHoVaH) Hebrew.
DEUS	Latin.
DIEU	French.
ADAT	Assyrian.
GODT	Dutch.
GOTT	German.
GODH	Danish.
GOTH	Swedish.
SORU	Persian.
ALLA	Mohammedan.
RAMA	Hindu.
DEVA	Sanscrit.
DIOS	Spanish.
ODIN	Scandinavian.
TEOS	Greek.
ZEUS	Greek mythology.
THOR	Viking.
AMIR	Arabic.
AMON	Egyptian.
PAPA	Inca.
ATON } ADNJ	Canaanish.
AGLA	Cabalistic.
INCA	Quechua.
BAAL	Phoenician.
ISTR	Persian.
DEUS	Portuguese.
ILLU	Syrian.
ELAH	Aramaic.
KAMI } SHIN	Japanese.
HAKK } ILAH } EZID	Hindustani.
NEBO	Chaldean.
BRAM	Aryan

DAVID RICE ATCHISON WAS PRESIDENT OF THE UNITED STATES . . . and slept through his term of office.

This unusual circumstance came about because the inauguration day of Zachary Taylor as President fell on Sunday, March 4, 1849.

President Polk's term expired at the same time. However, Taylor did not take the oath of office until the next day—Monday, March 5th.

In the meantime, David Rice Atchison—as President pro tempore of the Senate—became the chief magistrate of the nation between the time of Polk's retirement and Taylor's inauguration.

This period came immediately after a very trying session in the Senate, and Senator Atchison always said that he slept all during his term as President.

21

THE RIVER OF VINEGAR
(RIO VINAGRE OF COLOMBIA)
CONTAINS SULPHURIC ACID AND HYDROCHLORIC ACID
AND IS SO SOUR THAT NO FISH CAN LIVE IN IT

THE BOY WITH OWL EYES !
GIOVANNI GALANTI, of ITALY
CAN SEE AT NIGHT BUT NOT IN THE DAYTIME

A LEMON
22 INCHES AROUND AND
WEIGHING 4 POUNDS
WAS GROWN BY
W. G. MICKI
IN LODI, CAL.,
June, 1928

JIMMY JOHNSTON (San Francisco, 1913) STOLE 124 BASES IN ONE SEASON

THE RIVER OF VINEGAR

THE Vinegar River (El Rio Vinagre) is found in Colombia in the vicinity of the active volcano Puracé. It is really a part of the Cauca River which rises in the southern part of the country near Ecuador and flows 680 miles north to the Magdalena.

The high acidity of the river is in part attributed to the proximity of the volcano. It contains eleven parts of sulphuric acid and nine parts of hydrochloric acid in every thousand, and is so sour that no fish can live in it.

* * *

THE BOY WITH OWL EYES

GIOVANNI GALANTI, the sixteen-year-old Italian boy who has a peculiar affliction of his eyes which permits him to see at night but not in the day, attracted considerable attention during the month of April, 1928, when he tried to enter this country from Italy. The public health inspectors pronounced the youth a victim of Retinochoraiditis—the scientific term for "Day Blindness," and refused to give him permission to land.

The boy's parents live in Hermine, Pa.

* * *

THE BASE-STEALING RECORD

JIMMY JOHNSTON stole 124 bases in one season—the modern record. However, Johnston compiled this high mark with San Francisco in the Pacific Coast League where the season is long. Johnston played in 201 games.

This prize-pilfering performance resulted in Johnston's going up to the major leagues where he was a star for a number of years with Brooklyn. He is now manager of the Chattanooga Club in the Southern League.

ONE HUNDRED YEARS—AND A DAY

THE first hundred years are the hardest, it is said, and Jean Baptiste Mouron, of Toulon, should know. He served a full sentence of "100 years and a day" as a galley slave!

Jean Baptiste Mouron of Toulon was a flaming youth. In 1684, when but 17 years of age, he was convicted of incendiarism and sentenced to the depths of a galley ship to slave his life away. Exactly one hundred years and a day later, a tottering old man shambled unsteadily ashore in the town of Toulon. It was Mouron. He had served his sentence in full—and the world was even with him once more.

It was the common practice of the Mediterranean countries to use convicts to man the oars of their galleys of war. However, Jean Baptiste did not pull an oar for long, as the use of galleys for war purposes had practically ceased at the time of his incarceration. The ships were moored as prison hulks in the different harbors—principally at Marseilles and Toulon, and Mouron was chained to a bench below the decks and left to rot with the ship.

They made the old man like it. Even as Bonnivard did the dungeon of Chillon, Mouron learned to love despair; and years later when Louis XV. suggested that he might go free, the gallant old "galérien" refused to leave his "Hermitage" until one day after a hundred years had passed.

> "My very chains and I grew friends,
> So much a long communion tends
> To make us what we are:—even I
> Regained my freedom with a sigh."

And he died 6 years after.

Ref.: Memoirs of a Protestant, by Jean Marteilhes.

* * *

THE FIRST HUNDRED CENTURIES ARE THE HARDEST

THE first hundred centuries will be harder still, no doubt. At the present time there is a man in jail in Mainz, Germany, attempting to serve out a sentence of 14,975 years.

Otto Nodling, a brewer, was recently found guilty of violating the tax laws in connection with his brewery and was sentenced to pay a fine of 82,000,000 marks with the alternative of a day in jail for every 15 marks of the fine unpaid.

Brewer Nodling declared his inability to pay, and was taken into custody in December, 1927.

He has only about 150 centuries more to serve.

CONVICTED OF KILLING HIMSELF

PAUL HUBERT was convicted of first degree murder by a "Cour Correctionelle" of Bordeaux, France, and sentenced to death. The sentence was commuted to lifelong imprisonment and he was sent to the French penal colony in Guiana.

In 1860, after he had served 21 years in solitary confinement, the Procureur Imperial moved the French Cour de Cassation to review the case. The case was reopened and Hubert acquitted after the highest French Court found that his supposed victim was none other than himself!

The Hubert case is a "cause célèbre," and a great argument for those who strive to abolish capital punishment.

*　　*　　*

THE STING OF DEATH

FRANÇOIS DE CIVILLE was declared dead in 1562 and was buried. Six hours later—on the intuition of his brother—he was disinterred and revived. He lived seventy years longer, dying at the age of 105 from a cold contracted while "serenading the lady of his heart all night long."

From his tombstone in the cemetery of Milano.

*　　*　　*

THE MAN WHO HANGED HIMSELF

RADFORD WILLIAMS, an Englishman, was convicted of murder and sentenced to be hanged. He mounted the scaffold with firm step, and as a last request, asked to be permitted to spring the death trap himself. He did.

He was buried at the conflux of four roads in the center of London with a stake driven through his heart, "and over him drives forever the uproar of unresting London."

*　　*　　*

LIFE IS LIKE THAT

There are 68 deaths a minute, 97,920 daily, and 35,740,800 annually.

YOU CAN SEE BOTH
THE PACIFIC AND ATLANTIC OCEANS
FROM THE TOP OF MT. IRAZU
Costa Rica

DUKE FARRELL
THREW OUT 8
PLAYERS TRYING
TO STEAL —
in one game.

PAUL HUBERT
— of Bordeaux, 1863.
WAS CONVICTED OF
MURDERING HIMSELF!

HE SERVED 21 YEARS
IN SOLITARY CONFINEMENT
BEFORE IT WAS DISCOVERED
THAT HIS SUPPOSED VICTIM WAS NONE OTHER THAN HIMSELF

123456789
987654321
123456789
987654321
Plus 2
2222222222

27

"TO ERR IS HUMAN"—

"It is one thing to show a man that he is in error, and another to put him in possession of the truth."—John Locke.

Or as Josh Billings said: "The trouble with most folks isn't so much their ignorance, as knowin' so many things that ain't so."

THERE IS NO LEAD IN A LEAD PENCIL.

(It is graphite—one of the forms of carbon.)

THERE IS NO CORK IN CORK LEGS.

(The name comes from Dr. Cork who invented them.)

A GUINEA PIG IS NOT A PIG NOR DOES IT COME FROM GUINEA.

(It is a Rodent and comes from the western coast of South America.)

A BLIND WORM IS NEITHER BLIND NOR IS IT A WORM.

(It is a lizard and has two conspicuous eyes.)

GERMAN SILVER CONTAINS NO SILVER.

(It is an alloy of copper, nickel, and zinc.)

THE COFFEE BERRY IS NOT A BERRY.

(It is a seed.)

A PENTHOUSE IS NOT A HOUSE.

(It is a shed attached to a building.)

A STEELYARD IS NOT A YARD NOR IS IT STEEL.

(It is a regulator or balance.)

DRESDEN CHINA DOES NOT COME FROM DRESDEN.

(It is made in Meissen.)

THERE IS NO RICE IN RICE PAPER.

(It is made from pitch or wood pulp.)

THERE IS NO BONE IN WHALE BONE.

(It is Baleen, an elastic substance found in the mouth of a whale.)

THERE IS NO TEA IN BEEF TEA.

(It is an extract of beef.)

THERE IS NO KID IN KID GLOVES.

(They are made of lamb skin.)

A PICKAXE IS NOT AN AXE.

(It is a pick.)

TABLE SALT IS NOT SALT.

(It is composed of chloride of sodium.)

THERE IS NO SODA IN SODA WATER.
(It is water charged with carbonic acid gas.)

A CUTTLE FISH IS NOT A FISH.
(It is an octopus.)

PANAMA HATS ARE NOT MADE IN PANAMA.
(They are manufactured in Ecuador.)

THE FLYING FOX IS NOT A FOX.
(It is a large bat.)

HUDSON BAY IS NOT A BAY.
(It is an inland sea.)

THERE IS NO CHAMOIS IN CHAMOIS LEATHER.
(It is made from the flesh side of sheep skin.)

THERE IS NO CAMEL'S HAIR IN A CAMEL'S HAIR BRUSH.
(The brushes are made from the hair of squirrels.)

FRENCH BEANS DO NOT COME FROM FRANCE.
(They are grown in India.)

A TITMOUSE IS NOT A MOUSE.
(It is a small bird.)

WORMWOOD IS NOT WOOD—NOR IS IT A WORM.
(It is an aromatic bitter plant.)

THE LADY-BIRD IS NOT A BIRD.
(It is a beetle.)

A PRAIRIE DOG IS NOT A DOG.
(It is a Rodent.)

A WHALE IS NOT A FISH.
(It is a Mammal. A Whale is warm-blooded, and suckles its young.)

A HUMMING BIRD HUMS WITH ITS WINGS.

THE SO-CALLED FOUR ELEMENTS—FIRE, WATER, EARTH, AND
AIR—ARE NOT ELEMENTS.
(They are compounds.)

THE GLASS SNAKE IS NOT GLASS—NOR IS IT A SNAKE.
(It is a lizard.)

CHRIST WAS *NOT* BORN IN THE FIRST YEAR OF THE CHRISTIAN ERA

HE WAS born about four years before the period when the era began. A mistake in computation by a sixth-century chronologist is responsible for the common and erroneous understanding that Christ's birth was in the year I.

* * *

AESOP DID *NOT* WRITE "AESOP'S FABLES"

THE famous Fables were written by a Graeco-Italian named Babrius several centuries after Aesop's death. They should be called "Babrius' Fables." Some chroniclers declare that the famous Phrygian fabulist never lived at all. Anyway, the fables he is supposed to have composed are lost. Not one exists today.

Aesop's repute was wide-spread, and the term "Aesopic" is generally applied to all moral tales having animal characters, thanks to Socrates and later writers who made versions of Babrius's creations to which they gave Aesop's name, thus bestowing immortality upon one sage while robbing another of his rightful laurels.

* * *

NERO DID *NOT* FIDDLE WHILE ROME BURNED

IN THE first place the "fiddle" was not yet invented. Neither did Nero play any other instrument at the time because he was fifty miles away at his villa in Antium when the fire occurred, and did not return to the city until it was in ashes.

Tacitus, the historian, is the authority for this statement.

* * *

THE NEEDLE OF THE COMPASS DOES *NOT* POINT TO THE NORTH POLE

It points to the Magnetic Pole which is 1,500 miles west of the true North Pole.

* * *

THE SHORTEST DISTANCE BETWEEN TWO POINTS IS *NOT* A STRAIGHT LINE

Lindbergh proved that when he flew from New York to Paris. Lindy flew what is known as "an arc of the great circle."

30

NAPOLEON—LIKE MOSES—CROSSED THE RED SEA ON DRY LAND

PLEASE accept Napoleon's own word that he crossed the Red Sea *"à pieds secs"* (on dry foot). He says so in volume 1, page 2, of his *Mémorial de St. Hélène.*

The Miracle of Moses and the hosts of Israel passing over the Red Sea is a non-religious possibility. The point of crossing is near the town of Suez called Bahr es Kolzum (the Sea of Drowning)—Yam Suph in the Bible—and is only a mile wide and naturally shallow, due to sand bars.

The rise and fall of the tide is from five to seven feet. A strong wind blows northwest for nine months of the year, and often has a tremendous influence upon an ebb tide, causing it to vary three feet and more. (It is significant that both the Bible and Napoleon mention a strong prevailing wind.)

A combination of the above facts: wind, tide, sand bars and the narrowness of the Gulf of Suez would indicate that Napoleon told the truth. Besides, a number of Bible critics, both worldly and ecclesiastical, bear out his statement. I refer you to: *Biblical Encyclopedia* . . . under Red Sea; *Egypt,* by Bishop Charles Seymour Robinson, page 85, volume 1, and many others.

I have seen the point of passing myself. It is now about the same distance in width, but has been dredged out in a channel to a depth of thirty-five feet.

THE **WORLD**
WAS SOLD TO
THE HIGHEST BIDDER!
DIDIUS JULIANUS BOUGHT THE ENTIRE ROMAN WORLD
FROM THE PRÆTORIAN GUARD FOR $5,000,000
MARCH 28, 193

SELLING THE WORLD

AFTER the death of Pertinax the Roman World was offered for sale at auction by the all-powerful Prætorian Guard. Didius Salvius Julianus Marcus, a wealthy Roman merchant, outbid all others, and the world was knocked down to him after he paid the equivalent of $5,000,000 in gold on March 28, 193 A.D. The Roman Senate took the oath of loyalty to him.

When the Roman Legions stationed in Great Britain learned of the disgraceful deal they rose in indignation and, under the leadership of General Septimus Severus, hurried to Rome, where Didius was seized, deposed, and beheaded on June 2nd, 193 A.D.

Septimus thereupon became Imperator of Rome.

See any Roman History or Encyclopedia Britannica under "Didius."

THE GOLDEN MAN

"El Dorado."

How often have we heard that phrase. It means "the Golden," and was originally written "El Hombre Dorado"—the Golden Man.

And there is a Golden Man!

Immediately after Columbus discovered the new world a horde of adventurers streamed across the Atlantic to seek their fortunes. Columbus and his men had told wild tales about the lands that they had found and the wild army of Conquistadores that followed them expected to gather wealth with ease. These valiant old Spaniards came with no altruistic motives. They may have carried a cross in one hand but they held a sword in the other, and their motive was more a lust for gold than the love of God.

Among the first tales told them as they reached the Spanish Main, was the story of El Hombre Dorado—the Man of Gold. They were told by the Islanders of the Caribbean that there was a man of pure gold who lived in wondrous splendor somewhere to the south.

These Spaniards were told this story for several reasons . . . the most important of which was the impatient desire of the natives to be rid of these strange white men.

The simplest method of ridding themselves of the troublesome white men was to tell them about gold. Gold to the natives of new America meant nothing. Gold had no pecuniary value. To the natives of the new world gold was simply an ornament and they thought the Spanish crazy because this bright metal held such a lure for them.

It was a fetish, they thought, (and they were right) so whenever the bearded white men came down upon them they only pointed southward and hinted about the "Golden Man." They continually described El Dorado as easy to be reached and situated at no considerable distance. It was like a phantom that seemed to fly before the Spaniards and to call on them unceasingly. It is in the nature of man, wandering on the earth, to figure himself happiness beyond the region which he knows. The shining lure of gold glowed brightly in the darkness of this unknown land. A will o' the wisp.

But they were not altogether wrong.

There was a Golden Man! "El Hombre Dorado" did exist—and he doubtless exists to this day. The Guatavita Indians near Quito had a religious ceremony in which their King gilded himself with gold dust and went into a lake amid the mountains. Every morning before he made his sacrifice this ruler caused powder of gold to be dusted on over a coating of grease which made him shine in the sun like a true "Hombre Dorado."

THE WALKING HALF-MOONS

AROUND and around, in and out, but always upward goes the ferrocarríl of Peru. Soon the river in the Tambo valley comes into view—a strip of Eden amidst Sahara; a long brush-stroke of green on a barren canvas; a vivid testimony to the fatal fact that all Peru needs is a drink of water to make her domain a Paradise.

Upward and onward we go among the burning mountains, which have not tasted a drop of rain in a thousand years, until the highland desert of La Joya comes into view. Looking backward we can sometimes see the silvery sheen of the Pacific glistening in the descending sun some sixty miles away.

True As An Hour-Glass

Spreading before us are the famous walking half-moons of La Joya. They are crescent-shaped sand dunes ranging from about 100 feet in width to 15 feet in height, and of such exact shape that no human agency could make them mathematically more perfect than the constant winds of this plateau. This unfailing wind is the true explanation of why the dunes creep across the desert in a true northerly course at an even rate of fifty to sixty feet a year.

The wind, always blowing from one direction, blows the ashen colored sand up the convex side of the crescent from whence it drifts down into the hollow side in such perfect and regular fashion that the entire dune seems to creep across the plateau without a single variation in size or shape, and with a movement that marks the years with the same accuracy that an hour-glass marks the hours.

One has to look back but half a mile to see where a dune was fifty years ago when this railroad was built; and if you will look back five miles you can see where it was when the Inca sent messages to his people that strange white men with hair on their faces were coming up from the sea.

I am traveling the same road that Pizarro trod when these very dunes were miles back. How I admire that villainous old fellow! What a man he must have been and what audacious courage he must have had!

The Spanish government had dispatched two vessels to the little island of Gallo, off the coast of Ecuador, where Pizarro and his expedition had stranded, with implicit instructions to bring back every Spaniard they should find still living in that dreary abode. However, Pizarro was not looking for succor—but success! Drawing his sword, he traced a line with it on the sand from east to west. He turned to the south and said, "Friends and comrades, on that side are toil, hunger, nakedness, storm, desertion, and death; on this side, ease and pleasure. There lies Peru with its riches; here, home and poverty. Choose, each man, what best becomes a brave Castilian. For my part, I go to the south!"

So saying, he stepped across the line.

Thirteen followed him.

The boat sailed away, leaving this handful of men, without food, without clothing, almost without arms, without knowledge of the land to which they were bound, without a vessel to transport them to the mainland; here on a lonely rock in the ocean they remained with nothing but their avowed purpose of carrying on a crusade against the great empire of the Incas!

The glistening crescents of sand have traveled many miles since the days of Pizarro and his valiant crew—and they will travel many miles before we see their like again.

Thus Pizarro came down to Peru and robbed the Incas.

They were never satisfied—they always craved more. They starved, struggled, and suffered in their mad scramble, but in the end were no richer than before. Only one in five ever left Peru alive. Pizarro's share of the Atahuallpa ransom was 57,222 pesos of gold, but he was murdered before he returned to Spain.

A cavalryman named Leguizano was awarded as his share of the booty the Inca image of the sun, a huge plate of burnished gold. This rich prize was lost in gambling before morning; whence it came to be a famous Spanish proverb:

"Juega el Sol antes que amanezca." (He plays away the sun before sunrise.)

THE RANSOM OF THE INCA

Let me tell you about the ransom of the Inca Atahuallpa. It is as famous as it is fabulous.

From the hour that Pizarro landed on Peruvian soil and began climbing the Andes, the hand of friendship had been extended him by the natives, who regarded the Spaniards as superhuman. Pizarro repaid the Inca's kindness by inviting him to dine and then making him prisoner.

The INCA ATAHUALLPA
HAD EARS 15 INCHES LONG

Rip
drawn in CUZCO — PERU
"The City of the Sun"

THE FISHERMEN OF THE EL GRAN CHACO USE A PICK AND SHOVEL.
The Ophio-cephalous species of fish bury themselves in the mud
and the natives dig them out ....Brazil.

Atahuallpa was not long in discovering that gold was the object of Pizarro's visit to his land and in hope of gaining his freedom offered to fill the room in which he was confined with gold, as high as he could reach; and standing on tiptoe, he stretched out his hand against the wall. Pizarro drew a line along the wall at the height which the Inca had indicated and called upon him to make good his word.

The room was 17 feet wide, by 22 feet long, and the line was 9 feet from the floor. In one month this vast space was filled! The temples and palaces of Cuzco had been stripped of their glittering golden decorations. The wealth of this ransom has been estimated at twenty millions of dollars!

And then, instead of freeing Atahuallpa as he had promised, Pizarro ordered him burned alive in the public square of Caxamalca!

COMMODUS FOUGHT AND WON 1031 BATTLES

Commodus Lucius Aelius Aurelius, Emperor of Rome (161-192), was so proud of his records in the gladiatorial arena that he commanded the world to worship him as Hercules. He eventually met his death at the hands of a wrestler by the name of Narcissus who strangled him.

"LINDBERGH ... *Was the 67th Man to Make A Non-Stop Flight Over the Atlantic Ocean"*

WHEN I printed this statement in one of my "Believe It or Not" pictures in the newspapers not long ago, I was surprised at the reaction: almost immediately I was besieged with telegrams, phone calls, and letters—about 3,000 of them. Practically all of the doubting ones thought that "Lindy" was the first to make a non-stop flight over the Atlantic Ocean; and the few who did remember (strange, how few they were) that Alcock and Brown flew over, could not imagine who the other 64 could be.

They forgot two dirigibles!

Sir John Alcock and Sir A. Whitton Brown made the first non-stop flight over the Atlantic in 1919. (Newfoundland to Ireland.)

Later, the same year, the English dirigible, R 34, with thirty-one men aboard, crossed from Scotland to America, and returned.

In 1924, the German ZR 3 (now the "Los Angeles") flew from Friedrichshafen, Germany, to Lakehurst, New Jersey, with a crew of thirty-three men.

Lindbergh was the sixty-seventh.

PRESENT—BUT NOT VOTING

THOUGH dead for nearly 100 years, the dressed-up skeleton of Jeremy Bentham, with his head between his feet, sits in uncanny silence at the head of the hospital board around which the trustees of the University College Hospital in London gather. Jeremy Bentham founded this hospital in 1827 and presided at the first meetings of the Board of Trustees—and he still does to this day, although he died in 1832. Each meeting of the board has found his weird figure at the table. His gaunt form is erect, his sightless eyes stare outright, and his broad-brimmed beaver hat is never removed from the long locks that dangle down on his shoulders, nor is his gloved hand ever taken from the cane that it has rested upon for over 100 years. And as the various important bits of business come before the board, old Jeremy is consulted—and when no answer comes from his grinning teeth—he is recorded as:

"Present—But Not Voting"

This dressed-up bag of bones and dust of what was Jeremy Bentham sits at this board because the living Jeremy Bentham willed it so.

When Bentham died he left his whole fortune to the University College Hospital, but on the condition that his skeleton be preserved and placed in the President's chair at every board meeting. This unusual testament has been faithfully obeyed by the generations of trustees that have followed; and Jeremy still sits in the President's chair, and probably will never leave it until stones and bones have turned to dust.

Jeremy Bentham was a child prodigy. He could speak Latin, Greek, French and English at the age of five. Matriculating at Queens College, Oxford, when only thirteen, he won his B.A. two years later, and set out upon an eventful career that was to bring him fame and fortune as a writer, scientist, and philosopher.

His first work was entitled "Fragments on Government," which was acclaimed as a masterly attack upon Blackstone's eulogies of the British Government system.

Fame followed fast and the young scholar was soon taken up by the *intelligentsia* of his day and his works commanded attention not only in England, but on the Continent, and in America.

Although he traveled widely and led an eventful life, it seems that melancholy overtook him in the twilight of his life—he was alone and without a family—and it was then, evidently, that the idea of self-perpetuation came upon him, and the idea of always being present at the meetings of the College that he founded took definite course in his will.

It was in accordance with this last weird flare of his genius that his testament demanded that his head be severed from his body in the presence of his friends and placed in a separate glass case which now rests between his ankles, while a mask, a life-like replica of his living face, be placed upon his shoulders instead.

And so he has sat for nearly a hundred years—always present—but not voting.

PAIN? You don't know what pain is!

IF YOU think that you have suffered some, just read about Mr. Henry B. Smythe, of Maplewood, Mo., who has undergone 148 major operations! The game Mr. Smythe has suffered constant and painful invalidship for 37 of his 47 years. He has spent more than 200 hours on the operating table and is still smiling.

Moreover, he is a successful broker and manufacturer's agent, and lives happily with his wife. He walks briskly, works hard, and eats normally. Horseback riding and dancing are his hobbies.

Although there is a likelihood of many more operations, Mr. Smythe is undaunted. He will no doubt be glad to answer personally anything that you may wish to ask him.

* * *

I was traveling in Mexico a few years ago when I received the following letter. I print it just as it came to me.

Dear Gentleman:
 You make wonderful pictures. I am wonderful. I like to meet you please. I am

GUYAL VACA SEGUAL
The World's renown Insensible
FIRE EATER

I bathes, eats, and plays in fire. I eat fire, play with lead in my mouth. I take bath in gasoline and set myself in fire. I step in red hot oven and roast pound of meat in same to convince you and imerge as cool as ice.

I am King of Fire, the whip of fire.

I have been recognized by some doctors having not found any Chemical Substances in my body for I do not use them.

I am the only man that drinks hot lead.

I drink gasoline and light it in my mouth so that you can see the flames of fire shooting from within me, and I feel though I had only partaken of some cool refreshing drink.

I present myself as the only one can control fire. The man possessed of equal control of heat is yet to come.

I can also roll myself in red-hot coal fire. I will come to the hotel tomorrow.

MEXICAN GUYAL VACA SEGUAL.

I am the only fire eater Guyal Vaca Segual so don't confuse me with many performers doing the same work I do.

MORIMOTO...
Famous Japanese ... Can Swallow His Nose

A MURDER AT MIDNIGHT —
IF EVERY ONE WHO WAS TOLD ABOUT IT
TOLD 2 OTHER PEOPLE WITHIN 12 MINUTES,
EVERYBODY ON EARTH WOULD KNOW IT BEFORE MORNING

THE MURDER AT MIDNIGHT

THE HORNED MAN

HORNED men have raised the devil everywhere. The satanical and animal-like appearance of men with horns growing out of their foreheads have excited the emotions of the curious for generations.

François Trovillow, the Horned Man of Mezières, is famous to this day, although he died in 1698.

In Lhassa, Tibet, there is a man with a horn growing from his forehead to the extent of thirteen inches. The reflected glory of the golden sun bounces off K2 and Mount Everest on this curious promontory each morning as its bearer makes his obeisance to Gatama while turning a prayer-wheel.

The Horned Man of Africa, like the Horned One of the Himalayas, is still alive. I saw him in London several years ago. He seemed self-centered and satisfied, although black and a Christian.

Medical science is lacking in positive knowledge as to the exciting causes of horns on humans. It is a rarity that may be classed as a dermatological oddity. It is a skin disease called Cornu Cutaneum, a true horny cutaneous outgrowth varying in size and shape.

Although resembling animal horns closely, their anatomic structure differs in not containing bone and in having a cutaneous attachment. The Cornu Cutaneum shows preference for the hairy scalp and for the face, occurring occasionally elsewhere—as on the trunk, cheeks, glands, extremities, and even the eyelids! No part of the body is exempt.

I refer you to Rodriguez's extraordinary case, quoted by Croker, in which horns grew on the side of the head to the extent of twelve inches, and were fourteen inches around the base.

(*Diseases of the Skin, by Stelwagon.*)

THE SQUARE PALINDROME

R O T A S
O P E R A
T E N E T
A R E P O
S A T O R

THIS is the most famous of all palindromes—the famous Square Palindrome of the fourth power that has mystified scholars for hundreds of years. It is also an anagram of PATER NOSTER A O.

The famous Square Palindrome is found on the pavement of the sacristy of the Pieve Terzagni Church at Tremona, and is duplicated at St. Peter's Church near Capestrano, the Church of the Mother in Magliano, the Church of the Augustins in Verona, and several ancient churches in England and in France.

Its meaning has never been exactly determined. The medieval scholar, Panza of Italy, suggested that it may have been intended to express what wind and wheel convey to the reader of the Holy Scriptures, namely, eternity and infinity.

The latest of a long line of interpreters of this curiosity is a certain Mr. Williams of England, who succeeded several years ago in arranging the letters in a symmetrical way with the theory that the solution is:

"ORO TE PATER ORO TE PATER SANAS."

"We pray to Thee, Father; We pray to Thee, Father; Thou healest."

The literature on this subject reaches back 700 years.

THE MARCHING CHINESE

IF ALL THE **CHINESE** IN THE WORLD WERE TO MARCH- **4** ABREAST-PAST A GIVEN POINT THEY WOULD **NEVER** FINISH PASSING THOUGH THEY MARCHED FOREVER AND EVER !

(Based on U.S.Army marching regulations)

DAMNED CLEVER, THESE CHINESE

HOW did I get this one? How do I know that all the Chinese in the world—marching four abreast past a given point—would never finish passing, although they marched for ever and ever?

"Such stuff as dreams are made on."

Recently I dined in New York's Chinatown with Paul Fung, the Chinese artist. Much food and much talk. A real Chinese dinner has from twenty to thirty courses and lasts five hours.

It was late when I arrived home. Robert Warwick, who lives next door, yawned dramatically. "Hi! Ho! I'll be glad to turn in," he said.

And so to bed.

"Hi! Ho!" The words remained. And like the sixty-fold echo of Simonetta, they sounded again and again, until I was dreaming of the marching Chinese of Tsingtao whom I had seen so often trotting with their bundles on the Bund and chanting their invariable sing-song:

Hi! Ho! Hi! Ho! Hi! Ho!

Hi! Ho! HI-I-I!

They marched on endlessly in my dreams. They would never stop, it seemed, and did not—until the crack of dawn sent them all scampering off.

So I took a pencil and paper and figured it out, and drew the picture that you see opposite, which has astounded a lot of people.

This is how:

Although there is no definite information on the population of China, as a census has not been taken since 1403, let us take the reasonable estimate of 600,000,000 as the number of Chinese on earth. (This includes Mongolia, Manchuria, China, Tibet, Mayalsia, South Seas, North and South America, etc.)

Following the conduct of marches as ordered by the U. S. Army Field Service Regulations, the Chinese—marching four abreast, or platoon-squads formation, at the rate of three miles an hour for the average fifteen miles per day—will require 22 years, 302 days to pass a given point. A generation! There will be 26,280,000 passing each year.

Assuming that the birth-rate of the Chinese is ten per cent. (same as that of the Jews), and that half of these children die before they are able to walk, there will still be 30,000,000 new Chinese coming on each year to take the place of the 26,280,000 that have passed the given point.

And so they could march on forever.

In 1402 and 1403, the Emperor of China—using the death penalty as a threat—gained the only reliable statistics ever taken on the Chinese population. The census of 1402 showed a population of 56,301,026, and the 1403 census 66,598,337. This shows an increase of nineteen per cent. in one year.

The Chinese death rate has been officially determined only for the city of Peking, and amounts to two and a half per cent.

Ref.: *"The Numerical Relation of the Population of China," by Prof. T. Sacharog.*

METHUSELAH ... *Oldest Man in the Bible*
Died Before His Father

THE explanation of this is simple; Methuselah was the son of Enoch, of whom it is written:

"By faith Enoch was translated that he should not see death; and he was not found, because God translated him." Heb. 11.5.

48

COGHLAN'S COFFIN

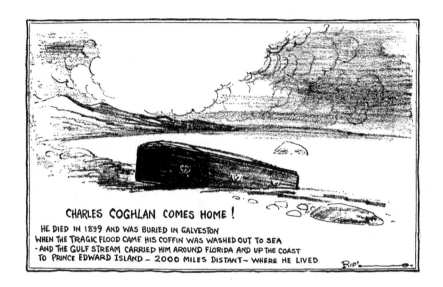

CHARLES COGHLAN COMES HOME !

HE DIED IN 1899 AND WAS BURIED IN GALVESTON
WHEN THE TRAGIC FLOOD CAME HIS COFFIN WAS WASHED OUT TO SEA
- AND THE GULF STREAM CARRIED HIM AROUND FLORIDA AND UP THE COAST
TO PRINCE EDWARD ISLAND – 2000 MILES DISTANT – WHERE HE LIVED

RIPLEY'S DRAWING OF C. F. COGHLAN'S CASKET AS CARRIED FROM GALVESTON FLOOD TO PRINCE EDWARD ISLAND STIRS ACTOR'S DAUGHTER TO SEARCH

By Charles Burney Ward

A WEST INDIAN hurricane, as the world still remembers, swept Galveston, Tex., September 8, 1900. As an incident of its tragic havoc it swept out to sea the coffin of the late Charles Francis Coghlan, famous actor.

Ever since that fateful day Coghlan's daughter, Mrs. Gertrude Coghlan Pitou, now of Bayside, L. I., has searched for her father's coffin. She and her husband, Augustus Pitou, who was once the late Mr. Coghlan's manager, have hired men by the year and spent thousands of dollars on the twenty-seven-year-long search. They received never a hint until—

Mrs. Pitou was reading the *Evening Post* of September 15. She turned to the sports pages. There, Robert L. Ripley's cartoon caught her eye.

"Believe It or not," she read. "Charles Coghlan Comes Home! He died in 1899 and was buried in Galveston. When the tragic flood came his coffin was washed out to sea and the Gulf Stream carried him around Florida and up the coast to Prince Edward Island—2,000 miles distant—where he was born."

This was news to Mrs. Pitou!

She showed the cartoon to her husband. Mr. Pitou, who is now booking manager of the A. L. Erlanger Theatrical Enterprises, read the cartoonist's inscription. Could such a thing really be possible? Mr. Pitou could not be sure. Neither could Mrs. Pitou.

CONSULTS CARTOONIST

Yet this was the first definite hint in all these years that either had ever had which would indicate the possible final resting place of Mr. Coghlan's coffin. "Hope springs eternal"—they would actively resume the search. They telephoned the *Evening Post*.

"What we would like to know," said Mr. Pitou, "is where Mr. Ripley got that information. We have never once heard that suggestion. I believe it's impossible that the Gulf Stream could carry the coffin all around Florida and up to Canada."

"Find out where Mr. Ripley got that," Mr. Pitou asked.

"Where did I get it?" Mr. Ripley replied to the reporter's question. "Why, two of the late Mr. Coghlan's closest associates have set down the incident in their published books. They are none other than Sir Johnston Forbes-Robertson and Mrs. Lily Langtry. As for the possibility of the Gulf Stream's carrying the coffin to Prince Edward Island, I checked up with a capable sea captain and several authorities on ocean currents, who say it's quite possible."

Ripley then cited Sir Johnston Forbes-Robertson's book, "A Player Under Three Reigns." In telling how he took the late Mr. Coghlan from his home on Prince Edward Island to play Mercutio in "Romeo and Juliet" in London, Sir Johnston writes (pages 165-6):

"In about a year, I think, he died at Galveston. Shortly after his burial there was a great storm came up from the Gulf which swept his coffin, with others, into the sea. The Gulf Stream bore him around Florida, up the coast, about 1,500 miles to Prince Edward Island and he came ashore not far from his home."

LONDON IS QUERIED

A like report of the curious incident is given in "The Days I Knew," by Lily Langtry, who appeared in several plays with the late Mr. Coghlan.

These sources of the report's origin were given to Mr. Pitou.

"It's strange," he said, admitting that both Sir Johnston and Mrs. Langtry had been good friends of his father-in-law. "But I'd like to know where they got it. Please," he asked, "find out Forbes-Robertson's source of information. This is not just a newspaper story to us. It's a very serious matter. If we thought there could be any truth in it we would start a search of Prince Edward Island."

The *Evening Post* sent a cablegram to its London office, instructing the representative there to get the facts from Sir Johnston Forbes-Robertson. The reply came by radiogram to the *Evening Post*:

"Forbes-Robertson writes, 'I distinctly remember it was given me by one in whom I had confidence. Indeed, I think two people told me the story. I take it that his daughter has consulted George Tyler, who was Coghlan's manager for some time.'"

OTHER REPORTS TRACED

George C. Tyler, theatrical producer, whose office, incidentally, is in the same building with that of Mr. Pitou, at 214 West Forty-second Street, said Mrs. Pitou had not consulted him, and added:

"I have heard that story of Charles Coghlan's coffin not once but a number of times. I was once his manager, and close friends of his have told me since of his coffin having been found on Prince Edward Island. It was washed ashore, as I heard it, at Fortune Bridge. I remember once, years ago, when I spoke of its having been found on the beach at Galveston, somebody corrected me—I forget who it was—and told me it had been carried in the Gulf Stream to the Canadian island. It has been told to me by several persons in whom I have confidence."

Charles Francis Coghlan was an Irish actor, born in 1841. He first appeared on the stage in London, in 1860, and came to America in 1876. He was leading man in a number of plays with his sister, Rose Coghlan, who was as famous in the profession as he. He also was leading man in companies with Mrs. Fiske and Lily Langtry. He died in Galveston, November 27, 1899, and his body was placed in a granite vault in a cemetery there.

. GULF STREAM GOES NORTHWARD

How that coffin might have been carried by the Gulf Stream to Prince Edward Island is a question which probably could long be debated.

Prince Edward Island, a Province of the Dominion of Canada, lies in a semicircular bay of the Gulf of St. Lawrence. Fossil plants, abundant there, and beds of peat, dune of drifted sand, alluvial clays and mussel mud, occurring in and near its creeks and bays, show evidence, many say, that they have been washed there from the Gulf shore of Texas.

The Gulf Stream, as oceanographers point out, flows northward from the Gulf of Mexico and follows the eastern coast of the United States to a point east of the Grand Banks of Newfoundland. It is narrow and deep, with a current that travels approximately eighty miles a day. It is joined by a current which comes from the West Indies and follows the same course.

Might Have Carried Off Coffin

In this connection, Cartoonist Ripley tentatively points out that, since the Galveston flood came from the West Indies, there might have been a backwash after the hurricane toward the West Indies. This possibly could have carried such a thing as a coffin out through the Gulf to the point where the West Indian current joins the Gulf Stream.

The Gulf Stream, when it passes a point between the Bermudas and the coast of the Carolinas, divides into several small ocean streams. And one of these streams, whose definite courses have not been traced positively, might well have carried Charles Coghlan's coffin to Prince Edward Island. Especially might this have been a destination for a derelict in the Gulf Stream, since, as is well known, derelicts in the stream rarely are carried to Europe.

THE HUMAN PIN CUSHION

THIS Hindoo ascetic, of Singapore, walked three miles in the blazing sun with fifty spears (each fitted with a very sharp point) embedded in his flesh. Imagine the excruciating agony that every footstep meant.

Why did he do it?

No difference. There is no sense in a Hindoo religious fanatic anyway. But the fact that he did it is interesting enough, and it all goes to prove how much torment the human body can stand under certain mental conditions.

THE LUCKIEST MAN ALIVE

SURELY he is Captain J. H. Hedley, of Chicago, who fell out of a plane nearly three miles in the air and then fell back into it again! Here is the account from Hedley's log-book and authenticated by Lieutenant R. C. Purvis, Recording Officer of Twentieth Squadron, R.F.C.

"January 6, 1918. Mach. No. 7255. Height, 15,000 ft. Lieutenant Makepeace, M.C., reports Captain J. H. Hedley accidentally thrown into air, afterwards alighted on tail same machine and rescued."

Lieut. Makepeace was a Canadian flying officer and Capt. Hedley was an observer in his plane when they were attacked over the German lines. In the running fight that ensued Hedley was dislodged from the plane when making a sudden vertical dive, and fell several hundred feet in a direct line with the machine—probably suction or a vacuum had something to do with it—alighted on the tail, and was brought safely to earth from a height of some 10,000 feet.

* * *

SILENT FOR 30 YEARS

REB FROMMER did not speak a word or utter a sound for thirty years. This remarkable penance was self-imposed. It seems that Frommer, in an outburst of temper, cursed his newly-wedded wife who soon after met with a violent death which Frommer feared was brought about by his abuse.

He was a celebrated local character of Czortków, Poland, and when he died in 1928, the newspapers of Germany and Poland repeated again the story of his life and of the strange vow that he never broke.

* * *

"3,675 FEET AND 9 INCHES"

This is a Sabbath Day Journey, the longest distance a Jew may walk on his Sabbath Day as prescribed by the Talmud Berachoth.

Orthodox Hebrews observe this Rabbinical rule to the present day. It is the Hebrew "T'hum Sabbath" meaning the limit of Sabbath.

Exodus XVI. 29; Acts 1:12.

THE SUN THAT RISES IN THE PACIFIC AND SETS IN THE ATLANTIC

IF YOU would like to see the sun rise in the Pacific Ocean and set in the Atlantic Ocean you must go to Panama. Only there can you have this unusual viewpoint—and anyway, even though you never see the sun at all, you will see Panama, which, I assure you, is worth the trip anytime.

The way to Panama takes you across one of the most adventurous pathways of the deep. A wonderful and picturesque procession of ships and men wended their devious ways among the islands and open waters of the blue Caribbean.

Santo Domingo was the birthplace of the Buccaneers. The island of Tortuga was the birthplace of the word "buccaneers." The true meaning of the word is not worthy of the men who wore it. At that time on Tortuga the principle article of food was the smoke-dried flesh of wild pigs—a product peculiar to the neighboring islands and known by the Carib name of "bucan," or what we call bacon.

As a result the inhabitants soon became known as "buccaneers"—in other words, "baconeers."

Among these islands, and not so far away, is Porto Rico, which is an American possession; and a little farther on is another of our islands—St. Thomas, where bay rum comes from. Near there is an island most famed of all, yet nobody knows it. It is the little cay called "The Dead Man's Chest." Of course, you know it:—

> *"Fifteen men on a Dead Man's Chest—*
> *Yo-ho-ho, and a bottle of rum!"*

But that was a long time ago—before prohibition.

Criss-crossing these limpid waters careened the "low, rakish craft" of the blood-thirsty free-booters—Morgan, Lolonais, Brasiliano, Portugues and Red Legs—and Captain Kidd who, by the way, was not a pirate at all but suffered the rightful penalty of one, while the murderous Morgan received the order of knighthood.

These wolves of the water hid in land-locked coves and preyed upon passing ships and Caribbean cities. They were not all low, rakish craft either. Morgan at one time commanded a fleet of thirty-seven ships—all mounted with guns—and with two thousand fighting fiends exclusive of the sailors. A tough egg in a hard-boiled world.

But all are gone.

All that remains is the chests of buried treasure which any one may find if he looks long enough. Many years ago William Phipps Salem, one-time governor of Massachusetts, found nearly two millions of dollars on Puerto Plata, which had been pirate property.

ONLY PIRATES NOW ARE AT HOME

The islands about and the lazy sea are now content to bask in the warm tropical sun and dream of the past.

The only pirates we have nowadays are in our own country—working as chauffeurs and hat-check boys.

But if you wish to see the sun rise in the Pacific and set in the Atlantic I suggest that you visit the Century Club in Panama. This club offers you an ideal view and a view of ideals, as it is situated exactly on the dividing line between two nations—the United States and the Republic of Panama. The Canal Zone is a strip of land five miles wide on each side of the Canal and running across the Republic of Panama. The Canal Zone is American territory and, of course, under the influence of Volstead. Panama, on the contrary, is under the influence of Bacchus.

The Century Club, which is situated as I have said, on a line between the two extremes, is divided on the question of prohibition also. The front door, which is in the Canal Zone—or United States territory, is dry; and the back door, which is in the Republic of Panama, is wet. Choose the entrance dearest to you—and walk, don't run!

But I really started out to tell you about the unusual rising and setting of the sun. In order to understand why the sun rises in the Pacific and sets in the Atlantic at Panama it is necessary to know the geography of the Canal. As you will note from the map, the Canal does not run east and west but from northwest to southeast; and the Pacific entrance to the Canal—Balboa, is farther east than the Atlantic entrance—Cristobal.

And as you sit on the veranda in the cool of the day—sipping your glass of this or that, you see toward the west a blood-red sun drop precipitately behind the verdant Cordillera—into the Atlantic Ocean! And if you should sit there long enough—until the gentle hand of dawn draws back the warm velvety curtains of the tropical night—you will see the glowing face of the sun rise suddenly up in the east—out of the Pacific Ocean!

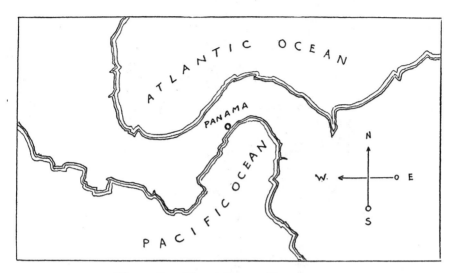

WHAT GOD HATH JOINED TOGETHER

The construction of the Canal is the greatest modern engineering achievement of mankind, but it was an old idea. Modern man is so full of the thoughts of his own achievements that he is inclined to forget that there is nothing really new under the sun.

Plans were made over 400 years ago for a sea level canal across the Isthmus of Darien. At that time Spain was by far the wealthiest and most powerful country on earth, and Indian labor was available by the millions for the cost of feeding them. The canal would have doubtless become a fact four centuries ago had not the Archbishop of Madrid advised King Phillip II. that:

"What God hath joined together, let no man tear asunder."

* * *

The two cities at the Atlantic entrance of the Canal, Cristobal and Colon, are the true names of Columbus. He never signed his name any other way than "Cristobal Colon."

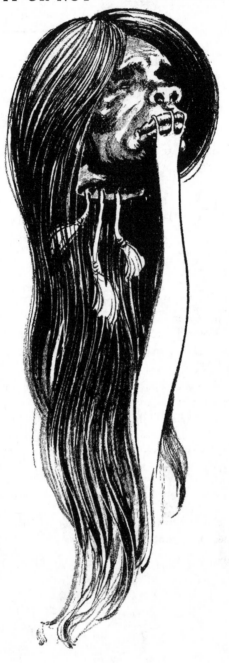

BOOTLEGGING HUMAN HEADS

THIS sketch was drawn from a human head that I bought for a little less than a hundred dollars from a bootlegger of human heads in Panama City. The head itself is now about the size of a baseball and the hair is 19 inches long.

A few years ago this head was an animated thing of normal size with a pleasant smile and sparkling eyes that sat atop the shoulders of a Jivaro warrior in the tropical forests of Peru. This happy warrior was careless enough to lose his life—and also his head which his conqueror cut off and bore proudly home where he proceeded to shrink it down to its present size.

Since head-hunting and head-selling is against the law, this shrinking violet disposed of his handiwork to a bootlegger who smuggled the grisly thing into the City of Panama where I was able to buy it.

The taking and shrinking of human heads is an ancient rite with the Jivaros, and one which has not vanished with modern times. It has, rather, been stimulated by the demand of tourists for specimens of the head-hunter's skill as souvenirs and all the laws against the practice that have been passed by the South American Republics are of no avail.

While there are traders to pay a price, and tourists to buy, the bootlegging of human heads will probably continue just as the bootlegging of hooch will continue in our own land.

The method of reducing and shrinking the heads remained a secret for many years and it is comparatively recently that anyone has witnessed the actual process. Friends of mine in Quito told me of a German scientist who ventured into the unexplored Pongo de Seriche—the land of the Jivaros—in hopes of learning their secret, and six months later a shrunken and mummified head with a red beard and light hair was offered for sale in the city.

The method used differs somewhat from tribe to tribe, but they generally proceed as follows.

As soon as a Jivaro has killed an enemy, he hacks off the head as close to the body as possible, and carries it away to a place of safety where he goes through an appropriate ceremony, and slits the scalp from the crown downward to the nape of the neck. Through this opening he flays out the skull, removing the flesh and skin of the face and scalp as carefully as possible. Throwing away the skull, he stretches the skin over a handle made of wood and then thrusts it for a time into a vessel of hot water which causes it to contract a little. Next a ring fashioned from a vine is sewed in the opening at the neck to hold it open after which hot stones are dropped inside. Magic rites are intermingled with each new process as the shrinking is begun by filling the head with hot sand and keeping it constantly in motion in order that it may act on all parts of the head uniformly. As the sand cools off, it is reheated and placed back in the head which is scraped each time with a headman's knife to remove the burnt tissues. Gradually, as the head dries and grows smaller, the Indian constantly works the features with his hands, pinching and moulding the face so that it will retain its natural appearance—and even its natural expression when reduced several times in size.

* * *

The Jivaros sometimes reduce and mummify the entire human body—but it does not seem to be commonly done. I have seen three. There are two in the Museum of the American Indian, Heye Foundation of New York, and the other was shown to me by Señor Juan Krateil, of Lima, who owns a doll-like travesty of Kurruba, a "Heroe Peruano," a quarter the size of the living man.

One of the two dequantitated figures in the New York Museum is a white man—a Spanish officer. This unfortunate old "conquistador" was searching for "El Hombre Dorado," the golden man, when he was captured by the Jivaros who reduced him from a living man of five feet, ten inches in height to a shrunken mummy thirty-one inches tall.

"Be Fruitful, and Multiply, and Replenish the Earth"

Gen. 1, 28.

LARGE families have always attracted particular interest among all peoples. In many lands the parents of prodigious progeny are rewarded by the state. Nations decimated by severe wars have used compulsory methods of marriage to gain children. The Orient is dotted with ribbon-bedecked shrines where childless wives pray for conception. There are savage tribes still existing who indulge in phallic worship.

Napoleon, when asked what France needed most, replied: "mothers." And a baby's crib once stood inside the door of the Cathedral of Notre Dame in Paris.

Roosevelt emphasized parenthood and especially honored the parents of large families. President Coolidge also receives with marked distinction the large family groups that call on him.

The largest family to call at the White House was that of Mr. and Mrs. Harrison and their 37 children. This healthy brood of young Americans seems very small, however, when compared with the multinomial households of the warmer and freer lands where wives are plentiful and can be had for the keeping.

* * *

MULAI ISMAIL THE FATHER OF 888 CHILDREN

MULAI ISMAIL, the culminating glory of the Sharifian Emperors, is the prize "daddy" of all time. He was a real father of his country if there ever was one. Mulai ruled Morocco for fifty-seven years with his capital at Tafilat. He had many wives as is the royal and Mohammedan custom of Morocco, and when he died in 1727, the stalwart old patriarch left living 548 boys and 340 girls.

* * *

Rameses II, the famous Pharaoh, was the father of 162 children—111 boys and 51 girls.

* * *

Rama V, or King Chulalongkorn of Siam, who died in 1910 had 3,000 wives and 370 children—134 sons and 236 daughters.

61

MAGDELAINE-CHARLOTTE-JACQUETTE-RENA
The nine-year-old mother

THE NINE-YEAR-OLD MOTHER

FOLLOWING is a true translation of the French Protocol as given by Dr. Cabanes in his book "Le Sixième Sens":

"After the sensation which the news of a nine-year-old child, seven months pregnant, caused in Paris and at the Royal Court, the personal Surgeon-Obstetrician to Madame la Dauphine (the French Crown Princess) consulted with the Masters of the Medical Faculty and then decided to take into his house, Rue Mazarin, one Magdelaine - Charlotte-Jacquette-Renaud, daughter of Louis Renaud and Magdelaine Laflèche, who on the 30th day of June, 1756, at 3.30 in the morning, was happily delivered of a male child through an incision made in her left side, and survived, thanks to the particular mercy of Providence. The newlyborn is well and in every respect like the child of a normal mother. He was baptized in the Holy Faith at the Parish of St. André-des-Arcs and received the name of Jean-Louis. A pension of 1500 francs per annum has been assigned to the mother, payable during her lifetime, and she will be placed in a Convent after her recovery.

"The unfortunate Garçon Marchand, who has abused the innocence and weakness of this young child died on June 9th, or he would have been amenable to the full severity of the law.

"The permission to reprint and to publish is given. Paris, July 4th, 1756, Berrier, Minister of Police and Royal Notary."

*   *   *

THE EIGHT-YEAR-OLD MOTHER

Clementine Aimée Pernon, of Puis Clos, France, 8 years old, gave birth to a perfectly developed child on June 3rd, 1866. *Annales de Gipsicologie, page 729, by Dr. Robert Gache.*

*   *   *

THE NINETY-YEAR-OLD MOTHER

IN THE "Chronique Publique dans la Revue Retrospective sous le Règne de Louis XV" (1742-1743) there appears an account of La Belle Paule Fieschi, of Rue de la Perle, Paris, who became a mother at the age of ninety. The child, a boy, was born on December 1, 1742.

*   *   *

Jean Baptiste Tavernier, the celebrated traveler of the 17th century, tells in his book "Travels in India," of seeing a Bhutan woman in northern India who had borne a child at the age of 82.

THE GREAT-GREAT-GREAT-GREAT-GREAT-GREAT-GREAT-GREAT-GRANDFATHER!

AH-KWEI, of Kansu, China, saw his descendants down to the tenth generation. He was presented to the son of the son of the son of the son of the son of the son of the son of the son of the son of his son! Ah-Kwei lived in the Golden Age of Happiness. And when the Emperor of China was searching for the happiest man in his Empire, the Kansu patriarch was brought before him.

Ah-Kwei had 130 living great-great-great-great-great-great-great-great-grandchildren in 1790.

Ref.: "A China Jubilee," by Robt. K. Douglas.

64

THE OLDEST PARENTS IN THE WORLD

MARGARET KRASIOWNA, of the village of Konin, Poland, died in 1763, aged 108. The following extraordinary circumstances are stated by Eaton as connected with the life of this woman:

"At the age of 94 she married her third husband, Kasper Raycol, age 105, of the village of Czywuszyn. During the 14 years they lived together she bore him 2 boys and a girl.

"The three children from their very birth, bore evident marks of the old age of their parents—their hair being grey, and a vacuity appearing in their gums, like that which is occasioned by the loss of teeth, though they never had any. They had not strength enough, even as they grew up, to chew solid food, but lived on bread and vegetables. They were of the proper size for their age, but their backs were bent, their complexions sallow, with all the other external symptoms of decrepitude."

"Though most of these particulars," adds Eaton, "may appear fabulous, they are certified by the parish registers. The village of Czywuszyn is in the district of Stenck in the palatinate of Sandomierz."

Kasper Raycol, the father, died soon after, aged 119.

* * *

THE GREAT-GREAT-GREAT-GREAT-GRANDMOTHER!

SPEAKING of descendants let me quote a verse on the tombstone of the famous Lady of the Dalburg Family who saw her descendants to the sixth generation. She was a great-great-great-great-grandmother.

"The Mother to her daughter spake:
'Daughter,' said she, 'Arise!
Thy daughter to her daughter take,
Whose daughter's daughter cries.' "

* * *

THREE CHILDREN IN THREE CENTURIES

PIERRE DEFOURNEL, of Barjac Vivarais, was the father of three children each born in a different century! The first boy was born in 1699, the second son was born in 1738, and the third was born in 1801. Each child was a boy, and each was born of a different wife. Defournel married his third wife when he was 120 years old and she was only 19. He died in 1809 at the robust old age of 129. The "Magasin Pittoresque," May 1877, has a reprint of the original birth certificates of the three children.

THE MOTHER OF 69 CHILDREN

MRS. Bernard Scheinberg died at the age of 56 after giving birth to 69 children. This remarkable mother lived near the German border of Austria and passed away about 20 years ago.

Not one was a single birth. Mrs. Scheinberg had quadruplets 4 times, triplets 7 times, and twins 16 times.

Mr. Bernard Scheinberg is still alive and married again, and what is more, he has had 18 children by his second wife who is also still alive. Scheinberg is hale and hearty and 77 years old and has 67 children living around him. He was the father of 87 sons and daughters.

* * *

The wife of Matthew Bauer, a farmer living near Nagykikinda, Jugoslavia, has given birth to a child each year for the last 28 years. All the children are alive and healthy. Twelve are married and 16 are still under the paternal roof.

* * *

BUSINESS FOR THE PIED PIPER

IN the quaint old town of Hameln, famous for the legend of the Pied Piper who enticed away all the children, there is an old house bearing a tablet telling of one Anna Roemer who made a lot of trouble for him.

It records that:

ANNA ROEMER
GAVE BIRTH HERE
TO
7
CHILDREN
2 BOYS AND 5 GIRLS
ON JANUARY 9, 1600

* * *

The largest family on record was that of Lukas Tchaffen, of Arlberg, Germany, (1612-1679) who left 1,091 direct descendants when he died. Herr Tchaffen had 5 children, 87 grandchildren, 446 great grandchildren, 553 great-great-grandchildren.

* * *

The family of Thomas B. Parker of New York City who died at the age of ninety leaving a family of 658 relatives, is noteworthy. Mrs. Margaret Sanger, the birth-control advocate, cites the huge family of descendants of Jukes, who had 1,200. Among them, according to Mrs. Sanger, were 130 paupers, 50 prostitutes, 60 thieves, 130 felons, and 7 murderers. *Nize babies!*

THE PROGRESSIVE MOTHER

MADAME de Maldemeure (Maldemeusre) gave birth to one child the first year, twins the second year, triplets the third year, quadruplets the fourth year, quintuplets the fifth year, and the sixth year the good woman bore six children. A total of 21 children in 6 years. She died as a result of her last confinement.

Madame de Maldemeure was the wife of Pierre-Roger, Squire of Maldemeure, a little village in the parish of Seaux near Chambelay, France. The first of their 21 children, Sieur de Maldemeure, afterwards became a notorious swashbuckler, courtier, and henchman of King Henry IV.

Dr. Ambroise Paré, the Father of Modern Surgery, is the authority for the above statements. He was the obstetrician at the birth of the sextuplets having been called into service by no less a personage than King Henry II, who had become interested in Mme. de Maldemeure's ever-increasing family.

Ref.: "Des Monstres," by Ambroise Paré, volume XXV of his "Oeuvres," chapter 5, and "Maldemeure," by Jean Cassaque.

*   *   *

YOU CAN'T BEAT THE DUTCH

Here is a translation of an inscription to be found in an abbey near The Hague, in Holland:

MARGARET, DAUGHTER OF THE ILLUSTRIOUS LORD FLORENT, COUNT OF HOLLAND, AND OF MATHILDE DAUGHTER OF HENRI, DUKE OF BRABANT, SISTER OF WILLIAM, KING OF GERMANY, BEING FORTY-TWO YEARS OF AGE, WAS DELIVERED ON THE FRIDAY BEFORE EASTER, AT 9 OF THE CLOCK IN THE MORNING, IN THE YEAR 1276,

OF

THREE HUNDRED AND SIXTY-FIVE BABES
MALE AND FEMALE

WHICH (IN THE PRESENCE OF SEVERAL GREAT LORDS AND GENTLEMEN) WERE ARRANGED IN FRONT OF THE FONT AND WERE ALL BAPTIZED BY A BISHOP, THE MALES BEING CHRISTENED THE SAME NAME, NAMELY, JEAN. AND THE FEMALES ELIZABETH.

ALL DIED SOON AFTER, AS DID THE MOTHER,
AND ALL WERE BURIED IN THE SAME SEPULCHRE.

THE LARGEST NUMBER OF CHILDREN A WOMAN EVER HAD

I HAVE been asked to state the largest number of children a woman could give birth to or ever gave birth to. A similar question was asked of the Editor of the *Journal of the American Medical Association,* and we reprint here the answer:

"Boer, and later V. Valento, reported a case in which eleven labors yielded thirty-two children. The patient was one of quadruplets and the husband one of twins. Berger (Halban) reported a patient who in twenty-five years had thirty pregnancies yielding thirty-six children, of which twenty lived. There were four twins and one triplet birth. The patient herself was one of twins. Burdach reported a case of twenty-seven labors with forty-nine children, of which there were six twins, seven triplets and four quadruplets. In a case reported by Küster there were forty-four children; in the first marriage, of twenty-two years, thirty children; in the second marriage, of three years, fourteen children (triplets, quintuplets and sextuplets). Geissler reported the case of Dr. Mary Austin, who in thirty-three years had forty-four children (thirteen twins and six triplets). She was an active War Nurse and had time to acquire a medical degree, too! A sister had twenty-six children and another sister had forty-one children. In Italian literature a case is reported of a woman who had thirty-three pregnancies with fifty-three children, and a forty-year-old woman who had forty-two children. A Brazilian woman is said to have had forty-four children, all singles, and her one daughter had nineteen and another eighteen children."

These seem to be authenticated cases but as the Editor remarks, even these seemingly authentic cases are doubtful, for it is hard to count sheep without a sheep-counter. The human memory is notoriously treacherous in such matters.

* * *

There are about 40,000 direct descendants of Confucius (551-478 B.C.) living in China at the present time.

* * *

Gorgias, of Epirus, was born in a coffin in which his mother lay dead for two hours.

* * *

Babou, Count of Abensberg et de Roye, had 32 sons serving in the army of Henry II of Germany at the same time.

* * *

Stephen Póździoch was the father of 7 children—each one born in a different country.

Marie Therese, Empress of Austria, was the mother of 16 children, of whom 2 became emperors and 3 became queens.

* * *

Neils Paulsen, of Upsala, Sweden, died in 1907 at the age of 160 and left two sons—one 9 years old and the other 103 years of age.

* * *

Bishop Heinrich of Luttich, Belgium (1281) was the father of 61 children.

* * *

Madame Jacqueline Montgaste, of Paris, is the mother of 17 children by 14 different husbands.

* * *

Hieronymus, of Rome, married 21 women—his twenty-first wife had had 20 husbands before him.

* * *

King Alphonse of Spain was born a king. He received the oath of fidelity at the age of one month.

AN INDIAN JUGGLER

AN INDIAN JUGGLER'S REMARKABLE FEAT

THE following account of a Hindoo who actually lifted a basket of snakes with his eyeballs was written by a young English army officer stationed in Deolai in the Bombay Presidency. He supplemented his letter with several small snapshots of the feat which was unquestionably an authentic performance.

"On my way out to India I heard of many strange and almost unbelievable tricks and feats which the native jugglers were alleged to be able to perform. Needless to say I took every possible opportunity of watching them at work, and saw many things which I could neither understand nor explain.

"I was stationed at Deolai, and shared a tent with Lieutenants Le Mare, of the 1st Royal Irish Fusiliers, and R. MacDonald, of the Yorkshire Regiment. To us there came one day a slim young native accompanied by a grey-bearded assistant, carrying a couple of baskets of snakes and magic paraphernalia. After the ordinary stock of tricks had been performed, such as the basket, mango tree, vanishing ball, etc., the juggler said in his broken English, 'Sahibs give two rupees, I show good thing.' When the rupees were produced the juggler took the larger of the two baskets, containing the python, and placed it upon a large cloth, the four corners of which he knotted together with a strong thin rope. At the end of this rope were affixed two little hollow leaden cups.

"These cups the man placed over his eyeballs in such a manner that a vacuum was created; then he shut his eyelids firmly over the outside of the cups, and, rising up from his former squatting position, he lifted the heavy basket containing the snake by the grip of his eyelids and the suction on his eyeballs alone.

"After the feat was finished and the cups had been removed, to the accompaniment of a horrid sucking sound, I examined the man's eyes, which were horribly bloodshot; moreover, he seemed to have difficulty in seeing for a few minutes, and the tears streamed down his cheeks.

"I have never heard of this feat being performed before or since but I vouch for its authenticity, for both Mr. Le Mare and I took several snapshots which I enclose."

"WORDS, WORDS, WORDS"

Hamlet, Act II, Sc. 2

THE English language is quite frugal with the letters of the alphabet as compared to the prodigality of foreign tongues. How the Germans do squander the alphabet!

What is the longest word in the English language? Who knows? Here are, however, a few that have posed for the time being as the longest words in the language.

The word most frequently cited is *honorificabilitudinity*, which is to be found in Shakespeare's "Love's Labor Lost," act 5, scene 1, line 44. To the Puritan divine Byfeld we owe *incircumscriptibleness*. Doctor Benson is credited with *antidisestablishmentarions*. To William E. Gladstone we owe *disestablishmentarianism*.

An examination of any treatise on chemistry will reveal several like these: *paraoxymentamethoxyallylbenzene*, and *tetrahydroparamethyloxyquinoline*.

Among modern German words of cumbersome formation is *Schützen-grabenvernichtungsautomobile*, which contains thirty-six letters to express what the English indicate by the word "tank" in its military sense.

There is also the "Turkish Association of Constantinopolitan Bagpipe Makers," which is designed in German by *Constantinopolitanischedudelsackspfeifen-machergesellschaft*.

Bismarck always spoke of a druggist as *Gesundheitswiederherstellungs-mittelzusammenmischungsverhältnisskundiger*. When he was angry he vented his spleen with this expletive—*Himmelherrgottkreuzmillionendonner-wetter!* *Damenmantelschneiderinnungskrankenkassenhauptvorstandsmitglied-erversammlung* is a nice German way of saying "Assembly of the all-highest direction of the sick fund of the union of female cloak tailors." And there is a club of Vienna called *Donaudampfschifffahrtselectricitaetenhauptbetriebs-werkbauunterbeamtengesellschaft*, which contains 81 letters.

You can give your tongue a rest by pronouncing this little Czech phrase —*Strc prst skrz krk*. That twister is literally translated into "thrust finger through neck."

This one should be easy for you—*Chrzaszcz szumi w trzcinie*. It is the Polish way of saying that "the bug buzzes in the reeds."

Here is the longest 12-word telegram. It won a prize in London in 1904:
Administrator-General's counter-revolutionary intercommunications uncircumstantiated Stop Quartermaster-General's disproportionableness characteristically contradistinguished unconstitutionalist's incomprehensibilities Stop.

* * *

A Revenue Agent in Germany is called by this name *Obertranksteuerdonativcautionszinsgelderhauptcassir* which may be literally translated "First Main Cashier of Duty on Drinks and Bail Rent Moneys."

* * *

Madame Schwartz, of Berlin, could understand a speech with the words pronounced backwards.

* * *

There is a river "Aa" in Pas de Calais, France. There is a lake called "Oo," and a town called "Oo" in the Dept. of Haute Garonne.

* * *

HINTERLADUNGVETTERLIGEWEHRPATRONENHÜLSENFABRIK-ARBEITERVEREIN

"Society of workers in the factory of bullet cartridges for back loading Vetterli rifles."

* * *

"PARAMINOBENZOYLDIAETHYLAMINOAETHANOLUMPHYDRO-CHLORICUM"

—ought to be in every medicine chest. Advertisement in a French newspaper.

* * *

Mons. Wzs is a native of the village of Ws, in France.

* * *

THE 1792 FAMILY

1792 is not a number but a name. The 1792 family is living in Coulommiers, France. There are four sons—and each is named after the months. January 1792, February 1792, March 1792, and April 1792.

March 1792 died in September 1904.

EPIGRAM UPON NOTHING

U O A O but I O thee,
O O no O but O O me;
Let not my O a mere O go,
But O my O I O thee so.
You sigh for a cipher but I sigh for thee
O sigh for no cipher but O sigh for me;
Let not my sigh for a mere cipher go,
But sigh for my sigh, for I sigh for thee so.

Composed by Rev. R. Egerton, Warburton.

* * *

CAN YOU PUNCTUATE THIS SENTENCE?

That that is is that that is not is not but that that is not is not that that is nor is that that is that that is not.

That, that is, is; that, that is not, is not; but that, that is not, is not that that is; nor is that, that is, that that is not.

* * *

"THAT" WORD USED 7 TIMES IN SUCCESSION

It is true for all that, that that that that that that signifies, is not the one to which I refer.

* * *

Enough of that.

* * *

Can you put a comma between—"The king and and and and and Queen"?

* * *

IT'S THE KATZ

THE oldest surname in the world is KATZ (the initials of the two words —Kohen Tsedek). Every Katz is a priest, descending in an unbroken line from Aaron the brother of Moses, 1300 B.C.

* * *

Short sentences containing all the letters of the alphabet:
A quick brown fox jumps over the lazy dog.
Pack my box with five dozen liquor jugs.

* * *

Machoumearobilengmonoolemongametsoarobilengmonoolemong means "99" in the language of the Bassoutos tribe of Africa.

HERE IS THE WORLD'S LONGEST CUSS WORD!
Next time you get mad, say:—

HIMMELHERRGOTTKREUZMILLIONENDONNERWETTER!

* * *

The longest name yet wished on a helpless infant was bestowed some years ago upon the little daughter of Arthur Pepper, a Liverpool laundryman. The child's initials exhausted the alphabet, and her christening occupied half a day. They called her Anna Bertha Cecilia Diana Emily Fanny Gertrude Hypatia Inez Jane Kate Louise Maud Nora Ophelia Prudence Quince Rebecca Sarah Teresa Ulysis Venus Winifred Xenophon Yetty Zeno Pepper. She was usually called Alphabet Pepper for short.

* * *

Ed Ek, of Brockton, Mass., owns the shortest name in the United States.

* * *

There is a city called "A" in Sweden, and a city in Wales called *Llanfairpwllgwyngyllgerychwyrndrobwllgerdysiliogogogoch.* I have been in a bay called "Y" in the Zuyder Zee, and on a Lake called *Chargoggagoggmanchaugagoggchaubunagungamaug* in Connecticut—which means in the Indian language, "You fish on your side, I fish on my side; nobody shall fish in the middle."

THE LONGEST WORD IN THE WORLD CONTAINS 184 LETTERS

This word is found in Aristophanes, Ecclesiazousae 1169. It means "hash."

*Lepado-temacho-selacho-galeo-kranio-leipsano-drim-hypotrimmato-silphio-
karabo-melito-katakechymeno-kichl-epikossypho-phatto-perister-alektryon-opto-
kephallio-kingklo-pepeio-lagoio-siraio-baphe-tragano-pterygon.*

* * *

THERE ARE 58,366,440 DIFFERENT WAYS OF SPELLING THE WORD "SCISSORS"—(PHONETICALLY)

The vocal (phonetical) value of the word scissors is S-I-Z-E-R-S.

There are 17 ways to spell the sound S in English.

"	"	36	"	"	"	"	I	"
"	"	17	"	"	"	"	Z	"
"	"	33	"	"	"	"	E	"
"	"	10	"	"	"	"	R	"
"	"	17	"	"	"	"	S	"

On this basis it is merely a question of mathematics to arrive at the stupendous number of 58,366,440 possible ways of spelling the word.

You will find "all the justifiable forms" of reproducing the 6 sounds S-I-Z-E-R-S in the *"Plea for reformed spelling" pages 35-39 by Alexander John Ellis.*

* * *

THE AUTHOR WHO NEVER READ A BOOK

PIERRE LOTI, on the occasion of his initiation ceremony as a member of the French academy in 1892, addressed his fellow members as follows: *"Je n'ai jamais rien lu. Par paresse d'ésprit, par une frayeur inexpliquée des choses avant d'avoir commencé je n'ai jamais rien lu."* (I have never read anything. Through laziness of the spirit, an unexplained fright of things before I start, I have never read anything.)

When interviewed by a representative of the *"Revue des deux Mondes"* in 1900 he reiterated this statement and called it "the only truthful one of all legends connected with my person."

H.B. APPLEGATE
— of Ogallala, Neb.

ANCHORED HIS BOAT AT ONE POINT
IN THE SAN JUAN RIVER AND
FISHED IN 4 STATES.
UTAH–COLORADO–ARIZONA–NEW MEXICO.

A COMPLETE COPY
OF "The Rubaiyat of Omar Khayyam"
5/16 OF AN INCH SQUARE
owned by
P.S. LONG
New York

SOVESKI
of Stanford U.
PITCHED A
NO–HIT GAME
AGAINST
THE UNIVERSITY OF
SOUTHERN CALIFORNIA
— BUT LOST.
March 29, 1928

SULTAN
HAMENGKOEBOEWONOSENOPAITINGALGONGABGURRACHMANSAYDINPANOTAGOMODE V
IS THE NAME OF THE SULTAN OF DJOCJOCKARTE

AN AMERICAN PALINDROME

```
N  O  M  A  D
O  C  A  N  A
M  A  D  A  M
A  N  A  C  O
D  A  M  O  N
```

Doc. Applegate.

* * *

ANTIPERICATAMETAPARHENGEDAMPHICRIBRATIONES

Is the title of a book by Rabelais.

"*Aldiborontephoscophornio*, where left you *Chrononhotonthologos?*" is a burlesque pomposo in Henry Carey's farce.

When traveling in Argentina, I met a man in Buenos Aires whose name was Señor Dɔn Juan Iturriberrigorrigoicoerotaberricooechea.

Pe Maung, in his "The Glass Palace Chronicle of the Kings of Burma," mentions the name of King Siritaribhavanadityapauaraanditasudhammaraja-mahadhipatinarapatisithu. His subjects were compelled to pronounce the entire 69 letters whenever they were permitted to address him.

The thirteenth holder of the title of "Living Budha," or Dalai Lama, oɪ Lhassa, Tibet, was called "Ahwangloputsangtoputanchiatachichiawangchu-chuehlelangschieh." This name was comparatively easy for his worshipers as it only contains 58 letters.

Mark Twain speaks of a Holy Man in Benares, India, who had 109 names —the last of which contained 58 letters. He writes it this way Sri 108 Matparamahansaparivrajakacharyaswamibhaskaranandasaraswati.

* * *

A little Honolulu lady bears this appellation: Miss Kalani Kaumehameha-kahikikalanynakawahinekuhao.

The late Western Empress Dowager, of China, that ancient Dame who hated the "Foreign Devils" with such celestial severity, was named: Tzu-hsi-tuan - yu - kang - hsi - chao - yu - chuang - cheng - shou - kung - chin - hsien - chung - hsi-huang-tai-hou. A careful count reveals 72 letters—all important.

If the old Chinese Empress possessed the longest appellation, then just as surely does one of her many millions of subjects possess the shortest of all names. Meet Mr. "I," of Hangchow, China. Philologists all declare this name the shortest as it is only one letter long and that letter displaces less space than any other in the alphabet. Mr. I is a graduate of the Johns Hopkins Medical School in Baltimore.

ELIJAH — GAON of VILNA

THE MENTAL MARVEL

ELIJAH, THE GAON, Chief Rabbi of Lithuania, possessed such a prodigal memory that he never forgot a book once he read it. Prof. Graetz, noted contemporary historian, states that the Gaon committed to memory 2,500 volumes. He knew by heart the Bible, Midrash, Mekilta, Sifre Tosefta, Seder Olam, the Talmuds (Babylonian and Jerusalmi), the Zohar, the Code, Rashi, Rambam, etc. and could quote any passage at will.

This venerable scholar resided in Vilna, the ancient capital of Lithuania, which at the time was the largest Jewish settlement in the world. His memory is revered to the present day by the Jews of Eastern Europe, and the above ancient print of the Gaon is prominently displayed on the Eastern wall of almost every orthodox dwelling.

HOT LIPS

BEAUTY, of course, is a matter of personal opinion, but surely nowhere in the world do people have stranger opinions than among the Saras-Djinges in Africa. The distorted lips of these Central-Africa belles are one of the most astonishing customs in the world. Their lips are pierced with wooden discs of increasing size until the lower lip is distended to such an extent that 14-inch soup plates can be worn. The enormous overgrowth of lip makes chewing of food impossible, so these women must live almost entirely upon a liquid diet. Speech is almost impossible and so difficult that they do not make anything but the most necessary splutters.

When a girl is about four years old her future husband makes a hole in the centers of her upper and lower lips with a rough knife and small pegs of wood are placed within. Gradually the size of the wooden pegs are increased until by the time she has reached womanhood her lips are things of beauty and a joy forever.

At night the Djinges wife sleeps with her huge lower lip on her husband's shoulder. This enables him to feel sure that his wife is with him, that she has not been stolen, or run away from him in the darkness.

PILLAR SAINTS

A MAN may be too foolish for his own good—but not for mine. Their folly is my fortune. I'll get rich off the ridiculous yet. As long as they have 'Bunion Derbies,' Marathon Dances, Non-Stop Coffee Drinkers, and Pole-Sitters, the "Believe It or Not" business will prosper.

For instance, if someone had told you some time ago that a man in his right mind would climb a pole and sit on top of it for more than two weeks without once descending you most likely would not believe it.

Of course you know better now. You have grown accustomed to that particular and peculiar swarm of Koo-Koo birds who have been infesting the flag poles of our nation for some time past.

"Shipwreck" Kelly began it with a well-sat record of 12 days and 12 hours. "Spider" Haines clambered up a pole in Denver and stayed there four days longer than "Shipwreck Kel." Soon all the available flag-poles in the country were inhabited. The city of Los Angeles was topped by a girl—even the air is elevating out there. Miss Bobby Mack, age 21, perched herself aloft for nearly three weeks.

I am not quite sure which one of these nuts is the nuttiest—but I think "Hold 'Em" Joe Powers, of Chicago, who stayed on top of the Morrison Hotel flag pole, 637 feet above Randolph Street, for 16 days, 2 hours and 35 minutes, is deserving of the crown of razzberries—or whatever they give the winners of sitting contests.

Let me add a comment from a Chicago paper just to give you an idea of fun at top-mast.

(Chicago Tribune Press Service) Chicago, July 16.—"Hold 'Em" Joe Powers, a dusty, dirty, frazzly, frowzy creature, came down from his flagpole.

Six teeth were gone; his legs were swollen; little needles of nerves burned into the soles of his feet when he tried to walk; his hair was snarled and matted; his beard was long; his face was black; his neck was sunburned.

But life had its compensations.

Joe had the memory of a record sixteen days, two hours and thirty-odd minutes on top of the flagpole which is on top of the roof which is on top of the tower which is on top of the Morrison Hotel.

But no matter what you do, whether it is sitting on top of a flag pole or on a tack there seems to be someone who has done you one better at some time or other. Now Sitting Joe and "Shipwreck" Kelly to all intents and purposes did some tall sitting; but I have seen better!

I saw a man who had been sitting on a bed of sharp spikes for 18 years. (I have already told you about him on page 9.)

SIMON OF THE PILLAR

And there was that man Savan. Savan's sitting amounted to something. He is the only sitter that I have ever heard of that had a practical idea behind him—or I should say under him. Savan was a soldier in Napoleon's army in Egypt. He went AWOL or something. You know the women out there all wear veils and maybe Savan got curious. The veil is the great beauty secret of the Orient. The heavier the veil the greater the beauty. I haven't the same faith in Oriental beauty since I have been out there. And particularly since I discovered that Cleopatra was fat and black and 46 years old and married to her brother when she met Mark Antony, who was 60 himself and wore a full set of whiskers. But as I was saying, Savan was ordered to do K.P. work but demurred. Nap called him in and asked him "Qu'est ce que ça?"

"I am not able to work," said Savan. "I am too weak to do anything more than just sitting around." So they took him at his word and gave him just such a job. They fixed up a nest of hen's eggs and placed Savan on it— and kept him sitting there, mad as a wet hen, until he hatched 3 broods of chickens!

But a word about Simon. Here was a man who really could sit. They called him Simon of the Pillar. Maybe he was a forefather of the illustrious Simple Simon of nautical fame. But Simon could sit. He was a Syrian ascetic who sat on top of a marble column in Alexandria for 69 years—without descending one time. Simon clambered up the column when a young boy and remained seated on this narrow space of less than 3 feet in diameter until his death years later.

This man belonged to a school of "Pillar-Saints"—a class of ascetics who sat atop various columns or rocks in the Near East, in the expectation of catching the first glint of the second coming of Christ, in the 5th and 6th centuries.

St. Simon the Elder, who is the subject of Tennyson's "St. Simon Stylites" (he spent 37 years sitting on top of a column) and St. Simon the Younger who remained aloft for 69 years, are the two best known.

During my several trips to Egypt and Syria I saw many standing columns, especially around Antioch, and they all bore some kind of a legend about some such "Saint" or other, who sat atop them for various lengths of time.

Food and drink were passed up to them, and the climate, as you know, is very mild in the Near East.

I refer you to the following books: "Die Säulen Heiligen im Arabischen," by Dr. Ignatz Weinzieher; "St. Simon Stylites," by René Aldoni; "Stylites or Pillar Saints," by Herbert Thurston.

TWO SCANDINAVIANS ROWED ACROSS THE ATLANTIC OCEAN

JUST thirty years ago two Norwegians rowed—actually *rowed*—across the Atlantic from New York. They made no great fuss about it. They were in New York. The weather was fine. They reckoned that they would row home and see how the old folks were getting on. Of course one ought to have a good, reliable rowing-boat, not a second-hand craft, so, like most wise cockleshell cruisers, they built her themselves, of well and truly seasoned cedar-wood. Eighteen ft. long was she, clinker built, with a 5-ft. beam and a depth inside of 35 in. *Fox* was her name. She dropped down the river from New York, on the outgoing tide, at five o'clock on the afternoon of June 6, 1896.

For more than a month the life of the rowers was relatively uneventful. The sun shone. The hills of swell went rolling majestically by. The oars were steadily plied, shift after shift. One ate. One sang. One slept.

Then things began to happen and their trip the rest of the way was a nightmare. God was good to them, however, and eventually they made the port of Havre where they landed sixty-two days after leaving New York. By examining their log-book and talking with them, Dr. Chancellor, the at first openly sceptical American consul at that port, ascertained that this astounding feat had indeed been accomplished.

WEDDED FOR 147 YEARS

ALL records for a long and happy wedded life belong to Janos Roven and his good wife Sara. They lived together as man and wife for 147 years—and almost saw their third golden jubilee.

Janos and Sara were born in the little village of Stradova, Comitat (County) Casanseber, Banat (Province) of Temesvar, Hungary; and they both died there—Janos being 172 years old and Sara, 164.

The aged couple attracted considerable attention during the later years of the wedlock, and the Dutch envoy in Vienna visited them and had their pictures painted. This painting is now in the possession of William Bosville, the trustee of the Earl of Northumberland, who also has the original documents of their marriage.

Janos and Sara died almost on the same day in 1825. Their son, aged 116 years, and his two great-great-grandsons, were at the bedside.

THE LAND OF THE HUMMING BIRDS

EARLY one morning—Oh! earlier than one wants to get up in indolent weather—we approached La Boca del Dragon—the Mouth of the Dragon, and squeezed in among the teeth-like islands onto the peaceful bosom of placid Paria and slid silently and quietly down along the ever-green shore of Trinidad.

"*Rocklets of ocean, so bright in your green,*
Bosomed on Paria's stormless breast,
How many mem'ries of times that have been
Linger around ye, sweet Isles of the West."

Trinidad!—"The Trinity." So named by Columbus when he first sighted it—not only on account of its formation, but in fulfillment of a vow he had made when in dire distress on the unknown sea with his wine, water, and food all gone.

Since we have all the wine and food we want (and we can get water) I prefer the appellation "Iere" as the Caribs called it—the "Land of the Humming Birds"—a well-merited name from the myriads of winged gems that fly like glowing sparks in the deep green forests that pile up so picturesquely on the starboard. Glittering Paradise!

Nature is nowhere more charming than on this warm, sweet isle. My arborist friend tells me that among the effulgent efflorescence of Iere there grows the *Tecoma Serratifolia*—the *Borassus Flabelliformis*, the *Corypha Umbracilifera*—the *Pithecolobium Saman*, and the *Couroupita Guianesis*. But they are rare and beautiful just the same.

Columbus and Raleigh wrote home to their girl friend, Isabella, about "the oesters that grew on trees; crabs that climbs their branches; trumpet fish that tooted their own fish horns; and about the Cascadura fish that wor a coat of mail."

Isa only laughed and said "Creelo ó no."

And I suppose you will say so too when I tell you about the Burning Birds of Huevos. Huevos is that little egg-shaped island off toward Venezuela where there is a cave full of whirring birds that suck goats and grow so fat that the natives of Paria stick wicks through them and use them for candles.

We were only 10 degrees from the equator—that magic line where nature is the strongest and man is the weakest. Here the earth grows vigorous and man grows lazy. The land turns green and the people turn black.

Kipling said something about East is East and West is West and never the twain shall meet, but Rud forgot about the Port of Spain. East Indians and West Indians meet and mix. The island is one-third Hindoo and the mixture is well seasoned with Chinese, Japs, Syrians wearing their turbans and saroongs, shirts and pants. The singular Singhalees and the Trinadadians act like brothers under their black skins.

I returned at night from the Pitch Lake—the "wonder" of the island—a lake of pitch of more than 100 acres furrowed by deep fissures of cool water. These fissures are crossed by planks. In many spots the pitch is absolutely firm, but in some places one's feet sink quickly, and here and there the pitch is seen boiling. The lake is said to have sunk ten inches in fifty years. The lake is at present leased to the Trinidad Lake Asphalt Company, whose average exportation is about 200,000 tons of pitch annually. A chain of buckets carries the pitch along the jetty, at which lie the steamers awaiting their cargo.

The streets are lined with sleeping Hindoos who only fold up, bow their heads and close their eyes when the day is done. I accidentally stepped on a black toe peeping out from under a huddled figure in a darkened doorway and a low rumble issued forth. You see, every man's home is his castle.

Now I am sitting on the veranda of the Ice House with the two sisters from Ottawa. On the wall inside is a framed tag line from the old English song.

"Ours is a nice house, ours is."

So they call it the "Ice House"—"where the cool green swizzles grow." A "swizzle" is the best tropical drink in this hemisphere. It is made of rum, white of an egg, a lemon, sugar, nutmeg—and swizzled. Inasmuch as Ontario voted dry recently it is only fitting and proper that Ottawa girls and I should be having a swig of a swizzle on the veranda of an Ice House as the sun goes down.

How the sun goes down! Night falls in the tropics. There is no twilight. The blood-red disk down the end of Marine Square has just tumbled precipitously into the sea.

Now it is dark.

JIM CORBETT FOUGHT IN THE PRIZE RING FOR 18 YEARS . . . and never had a black eye or a bloody nose.

This fact is flattering testimony to the remarkable skill of Corbett. "Gentleman" Jim was the first great exponent of cleverness inside the ropes. When he defeated the great slugger John L. he revolutionized the game at the same time.

THE FISH THAT CLIMBS TREES

THIS finny acrobat that is wont to leave its aquaeous habitat to climb trees is a native of Malaysia. It is more formally known as the Periophthalmus Schlosseri. When the tide is out these frisky fish squirm playfully about in the mud and frequently wriggle up the nearby trees in quest of toothsome insects. They propel themselves with unusual agility by means of two strong leg-like fins, and are able to ascend good-sized trees where they sometimes look down on travelers with their big soulful eyes.

* * *

"Dear Rip:

Your "Believe It or Not" cartoons astound me daily, but I think that recently I witnessed a happening worthy of your mention.

I was fishing about a mile or so above Kalma on the Columbia River when suddenly I saw a Black Bass—weighing about 4 pounds—leap from the river and swallow a bird.

Believe me,

A. B. Stafford."

RED RAIN

E VERY now and then some section of the world goes into a panic over the queer behavior of the skies. Not long ago in Clermont, France, the provincials thought the end of the world had come. It was raining blood! At least they thought so; and there could be no doubt but that the rain was red.

Surely it was the end of the world. But in a short time the showers stopped and the old world went rolling on just the same.

There are no proven explanations for such showers. The rain was red, no doubt, and the best reason advanced for the phenomenon disclosed the fact that the air was full of red dust which was believed to have been blown over from the Desert of Sahara.

Wild stories of bloody rain have been related for ages, and it is only of recent date that the non-miraculous nature of them was determined. Homer, Virgil, and Plutarch mention blood showers. Plutarch speaks of showers of blood following great battles, and asserts that bloody vapors, distilled from the bodies of the slain, impregnated the clouds, from which they were subsequently shed upon the earth.

The most recent account of red rain was sent to me from a friend of mine in China, who clipped it from the *Central China Post*. There is no doubt of its authenticity.

RAIN OF BLOOD

MONGOLIA FOLK IN TERROR OVER PHENOMENON

Harbin, June 29, 1928.

A "rain of blood" in Mongolia has spread terror among the people and temporarily deranged trading conditions there, according to reports received here.

The "blood rain" coincided with an epidemic of dysentery and the Mongols took this as a sign of heavenly displeasure, fleeing terror-stricken in every direction and abandoning their yiurts and cattle herds.

The Phenomenon started with a rapid approach of heavy dull-brown clouds and a red rain then continued to fall for three hours, leaving the whole landscape, yiurts and cattle painted a deep red hue.

European traders who were present easily discovered that the coloring was due to red clay, which must have been raised skyward by a cyclone, but they were unable to persuade the Mongols of this.

For three days the terror lasted, the men wearing amulets of horsehair around their necks and the women each night placing infants outside the yiurts as an offering to God with the hope of diverting heavenly wrath from the rest of the occupants. As the nights were cold the wails of the infants ceased only with daylight.

RED
SNOW
FALLS IN
JAPAN
—

EMMETT FRENCH
PLAYED PINEHURST
WITH A PUTTER
IN 80

Jan. 12, 1921

THIS
LETTER
WAS
DELIVERED
64 YRS.
LATE

GLAEDELIGT NYTAAR
BOLDOG ÚJÉVET
FELIZ AÑO NUEVO
שנה טובה
GOTT NYTT 'ÅR
UNE HEUREUSE NOUVELLE ANNÉE
STASTNY NOVÝ ROK
GLÜCKLICHES NEUJAHR
BUON ANNO
WESOŁEGO NOWEGO ROKU
GELÜKKIG NIEUW JAAR
GODT NYTAAR
HAPPY NEW YEAR
ETC

THE BARKING BIRD

THE bird that barks is a red-breasted little fellow indigenous to central Chile, and is called by the natives *"Guid-guid."* It sounds altogether like a small dog yelping in the forest. A person will sometimes hear the bark close by, but in vain may endeavor by watching, and with still less chance by beating the bushes, to see the bird; yet at other times the guid-guid fearlessly comes near.

Ref.: Charles Darwin.

* * *

THE SHARK DESTROYER

WHO would ever imagine that a little soft fish—less than a foot in length—could kill the great and savage shark?

The little Urchin-fish, or Sea Hedgehog (Diodon Maculatus), of South America frequently destroys savage monsters 25 feet long, in a most peculiar manner. This fish, with its flabby skin, arrayed with spiny points, possesses the singular power of distending itself into a globular form, and thus causing the spines to project in every direction like the quills of an irritated porcupine.

When swallowed by a shark it calmly eats and bores its way out, not only through the coats of the stomach, but completely through the sides of the monster—thus killing it.

* * *

MAN-EATING CLAMS

I MEAN that this species of clams eats men—not that men eat the clams. The mammoth clams of Malaysia—measuring 4 feet across and weighing 500 pounds are sure death to anybody careless enough to step within their open jaws. I heard many stories, when I was out there, of natives who had lost their lives in this manner.

There is a giant clam whose shells are now used as holy-water basins in the Cathedral of St. Sulpice, Paris, which must have weighed nearly 700 pounds. The shells alone weigh 550 pounds and are nearly 5 feet across.

PRANKS OF NATURE

WHEN we consider how fearfully and wondrously made we all are, it is not surprising that Mother Nature sometimes makes a mistake. Human errors are not always pleasant to look at or think about, so I will not go into any length of detail discussing the mistakes or monstrosities of life.

THE CHILD CYCLOPS

THE famous Clement child of Tourcoing, France, was born (1793) with only one eye located in the center of her forehead. She was perfectly normal in every other way, and lived to the age of fifteen.

Reported by Buffon in his Natural History, Vol. II.

THE TRANSPARENT MAN

HSIEH HSUAN, a native of Yu-t'ien in Chihli, China (1389-1464) was born with transparent flesh. The bones and organs of his body were plainly visible.

Hsieh was a profound scholar and attained his Chu Jen Degree. He entered upon an official career, but became implicated in a bribery case, and was sentenced to death. He continued his studies in prison and calmly studied a book even when led out to execution. He was reprieved and later canonised, and in 1572 his tablet was placed in the Confucian Temple.

Ref.: Chinese Biographical Dictionary, by Herbert A. Giles.

* * *

THE CRAB-TOED TRIBE

IN THE western part of New York State dwells a community of crab-toed people whose peculiar affliction has puzzled scientists. The hands and feet of this group of people resemble claws of a crab or lobster.

Here is the report of the Superintendent of the Rome State School, of New York, Dr. Charles Bernstein:

> "The Rome State School sent a field worker into the community where this strange progeny existed and the descriptive matter showed that there have been 184 cases of crab-toes—most of whom were social outcasts in the community, presenting many alcoholics, prostitutes, etc.
>
> "It was discovered that an English woman came over in the year 1800 and settled in Western New York. Later she married and the male offsprings of this union were crab-toed. Later it was found that this was a sex-linked affair through which the females never presented the symptoms but transmitted it to their male offspring, no females ever having it but all females transmitted it to their male children.
>
> "While the intelligence status of these people is very low it is sufficient to enable them to become successful workers and often skilled mechanics. They do not seem especially sensitive about their situation as they readily submit to having their pictures taken, etc."

* * *

Bidault, a French peasant, was born with two noses.

* * *

Leone, the Athenian courtesan, bit off her own tongue to prevent herself from revealing the conspiracy between Harmodius and Aristogiton.

A statue in the form of a lioness without a tongue was erected in her honor by the Athenians.

YOGI HARIDAS

THIS famous Ascetic could touch his forehead with his tongue. It is a form of high Hindoo heroics. In other words Haridas could touch his caste mark with his tongue. This required years of practice and many painful surgical operations on the roots of his tongue.

* * *

General Townsend, of London, could control the palpitation of his heart and suspend its action entirely at will.

This unnatural phenomenon is attested to by the well-known English physicians, Doctors Cheyne and Bayard.

The General died eight days after suspending his heart action for half an hour.

* * *

Leach, the noted dwarf, (1789-1818) had arms so long that he could touch the ground while standing upright.

THE FORK-TONGUED FRÄULEIN

SURELY there never lived a more unfortunate young woman than this Frankfort Fräulein. She had two tongues but could not speak a word! Her case is reported by both the *Medical Record*, and the *Courrier Medical* of France. This peculiar mistake of nature is extremely rare although it has happened before.

THE GLASS SNAKE

THE glass snake is not made of glass nor is it a snake. It is so-called because of its odd propensity of snapping into pieces at the slightest touch. It is a lizard, but it is indeed so singularly like a serpent that it can only be distinguished from one by certain anatomical marks, such as the presence of eyelids, and the solid jawbones.

To catch a perfect specimen of the glass snake is very difficult business for when alarmed it has the remarkable habit of contracting the muscles of its tail with such exceeding force that the member snaps off the body. The snake will sometimes break into several pieces if struck slightly with a switch. It is found only in North America.

THE LEFT-HANDED FAMILY

THE family of Colombière, Nancy, France, were all born with two left hands—that is, both hands were left hands. This peculiarity was transmitted through the males; the females were exempt. They are perfectly normal in every other way.

THE MAN FAMILY

THE Bossant family of Gijon, Spain, have had no girls born to them for more than one hundred years. They are a large family but for some reason no girls.

* * *

John Sinclair, of Halkirk, Caithness-shire, England, was married three times, and each wife bore him ten sons. He died in 1890.

* * *

Vaclav Kratochwil, of Prerau, Czechoslovakia, has blue eyelashes.

THE FORKED-TONGUED FRÄULEIN of FRANKFORT.

GRETEL MEYER WHO HAD 2 TONGUES — BUT COULD NOT SPEAK.

SIEGMUND KLEIN
weight...146 lbs.
PRESSED
233½ LBS.
TO ARMS LENGTH
OVER HIS HEAD

H. HANSON
LOST A POUND A DAY
FOR 100 DAYS

LONDON'S HONKING PEDESTRIAN

HONK HONK

HONKS TO WARN AUTOS ASIDE

THE GLASS SNAKE
SNAPS INTO
PIECES AT THE
SLIGHTEST TOUCH

Rip's

97

THE HALF WOMAN

"VIOLETTA," as she prefers to be known, was born without arms or legs, of normal parents less than thirty years ago in Germany. She is a lady of perennial good nature—realizing that what one never possesses one never misses. Her body is well formed otherwise, she enjoys perfect health, and her senses of sight, hearing, smell, taste and touch are all developed and perfected in their separate and various functions far beyond the average normal person's.

Violetta's accomplishments in overcoming the unkindness of Mother Nature are astounding. She rarely needs the assistance of anyone, and is able to get about with remarkable facility. She can dress herself, comb her own hair, thread a needle, sew, and perform other feats apparently bordering on the impossible.

LIU CH'UNG

GOVERNOR 崇 of Shansi
AD 955

HAD DOUBLE EYES

THE DOUBLE-EYED MAN

LIU CH'UNG, or Liu Min, as he was sometimes known, was born with double pupils in each eye. This strange freak of nature did not in the least deter this active man. He became Governor of Shansi, Minister of State, and through intrigue with the Dowager Empress, had his son proclaimed Heir Apparent. He also loved wine and gambling.

I refer you to Herbert A. Giles' book on China.

* * *

THE MAN WITHOUT EARS

EZECHIEL EADS, of Athens, New York, who died in 1884, was born without ears. The sides of his head bore no trace of ears whatever; neither had he openings for ears.

However, he was able to hear through his mouth which he opened wide for the purpose.

THE FAMILY PHYSICIANS

THE Curtis family of London has maintained an unbroken line of doctors for 224 years, until September 25, 1927. Until this date there has always been a member of the family with an M.D. Degree. The last of this long line was Doctor William Curtis who died at the age of eighty-seven.

* * *

LION-HEARTED

The lion has the smallest heart of all predatory animals.

Philip II, of Spain, one of the most cowardly of all tyrants, possessed the largest heart of any known man.

* * *

Joseph de Mai, of Naples, was born with two hearts. He sold his own body to the English Academy of Medicine for $3,000.

* * *

Plinius tells of the child called Eutimenius who was sexually mature at the age of three years.

* * *

Magdalena Strumarczuk, of Tobolsk, Russia, had her breasts on her back. She was the mother of three children and nursed them normally.

* * *

Sophie Bunnen, wife of a Pomeranian farmer of Prussia, gave birth to eleven children in sixteen months. She had sextuplets and quintuplets. (1880-1881.)

Reported by Dr. Gottlob, famous German obstetrician.

* * *

Duke Leopold Eberhart, of Württemberg, married his seventeen children with each other.

THE DUSTY OCEAN

O H! Yes it is! The ocean is often very dusty. A recent account of a dust storm at sea was reported in June, 1928, by Captain Nemaru of the Japanese steamship "Montreal Maru" on arrival in Tacoma from the Orient.

Captain Nemaru stated that two buckets full of dust were swept from the decks on several mornings in succession, and that the dust powdered the passengers, decks, and lifeboat coverings.

A few months before, the Captain of the steamship "Justin" reported a sand storm in the North Atlantic ocean about midway across.

Recently the crew of the "Jaden," a Roosevelt Line steamer, came into Calcutta with stories of a dust storm in the Red Sea. The red dust or sand hung so thick over the ship as to make navigation difficult, and the ship was forced to slow down as though in a dense fog. The whole sky was obscured by a reddish haze of sand from the desert.

* * *

Darwin writes of the "Beagle's" experience off Porto Praya, Brazil. He collected several packets of the dust and had them analyzed by Professor Ehrenberg, who found that the dust contained no less than 67 different organic forms. These infusoria, with the exception of two marine species, were all the inhabitants of fresh water.

Darwin arrived at the conclusion that this dust had been raised high in the air and blown over from Africa.

* * *

The Monthly Weather Review reports Red Rain on the coast of New-foundland in 1890 (Vol. 29, page 121) and snowflakes 15 inches across and 8 inches thick that fell in Montana 1887 (page 73).

* * *

Black Rain fell in Ireland over an area of 400 square miles on May 14, 1849.
Ref.: "Annals of Scientific Discovery."

* * *

Red, white and blue hailstones fell in Russia, June 14, 1880.
Ref.: "Annals of Philosophy," Prof. Schwedoff.

* * *

The report of the Smithsonian Institute for 1870 (page 479) states that hailstones the size of elephants fell at Seringpatan, India.

RAINING FISHES AND FROGS

THERE are numerous accounts of showers of fishes and frogs—and even rats. And such things actually happened. A friend of mine wrote me that he witnessed a fall of fishes in the town of Longreach, Queensland, Australia, in March, 1924. "I picked some of them up and found that they were 1½ inches to 3 inches long, and very much alive."

Such showers are easily explained.

Tornadoes and waterspouts passing over bodies of shallow water are quite apt to suck up fish, frogs, tadpoles, etc., into the clouds, later despositing them at distant places along the path of the storm.

There are many cases of so-called miraculous showers in which the substances found on the ground did not actually fall from aloft. Thus some alleged rains of blood are due to the deposit of red fluid ejected by certain species of lepidoptera emerging simultaneously in large numbers from their cocoons, and others to the rapid multiplications in rain pools of algae and rotifers containing red coloring matter. The well-known red snow of polar regions results from the presence of similar organisms.

* * *

THE RED SEA

IN 1823, the waters of the bay and seaport of Tor, not far from Mount Sinai, turned blood red three times. This phenomenon is described by Darwin and Ehrenberg as being caused by a marine plant, the Trichodesium. This minute organism is also the probable explanation of the first of the Egyptian plagues mentioned in Exodus.

MANNA FROM HEAVEN

MANNA, the bread from the skies, that the Lord sent down to the starving hosts of Israel was not only a miracle but a scientific fact.

Believe me, for I have tasted of it myself. It is gathered by the Arabs today and sold to the tourists in the Holy Land. It is a resinous gum exuding from the fragile twigs of the tamarisk, an evergreen shrub, which is found in several valleys of the Mid-Sinai. The honey-like drops appear usually during June and July just before sun-up while the air is cold and dewy.

I found it sweet-tasting and gummy, but for the life of me I cannot imagine anybody growing very fat on it.

Recently several organizations have attempted to search out the source of this sweet somewhere in the shadow of Mount Sinai. According to the news from Jerusalem, it is believed that this Heaven-sent nourishment has commercial possibilities; so don't be surprised if in the near future we find these famous agglutinized tears for sale in every candy store.

* * *

WHISTLING TREES

If you would listen to trees that whistle, you must go to the melodious Acacia groves in the land of "Fuzzy Wuzzy"—the Sudan.

This freak of nature is caused by the larvae of insects which work their way inside the ivory-white shoots and cause them to swell out at their base like globular bladders to the extent of an inch or more. After this mysterious insect has unaccountably managed to glide out of its circular hole, this thorn-like shoot becomes a sort of musical instrument upon which the wind, as it blows, produces the regular sound of a flute.

* * *

SHIRTS GROWING ON TREES

Humboldt describes the "shirt trees."

"We saw on the slope of the Cerra Dnida shirt trees fifty feet high. The Indians cut off cylindrical pieces two feet in diameter, from which they peel the red and fibrous bark without making a longitudinal incision. This bark affords them a sort of a garment which resembles a sack without a seam. The upper opening serves for the head, and the two lateral holes are cut to admit the arms."

OYSTERS GROWING ON TREES

"Oysters growing on trees? Impossible," everybody said upon my return from a South American jaunt.

Yet the oyster tree, that is considered such a curiosity, is very common on the islands of the Caribbean and the Spanish Main. I have seen many such trees in Cuba, Trinidad, Barbados, and Colombia, with their lower stems and branches literally covered with the festive oyster. These peculiar shell-fish are found in lagoons and swamps along the coast, and they attach themselves to the lower parts of the Mangrove trees as far up as the tide will rise and the spray will fly. When the tide is out, the Mangrove trees, which, by the way, are one of the very few trees that flourish in salt water, present a strange appearance with their oyster crop.

* * *

THE COW TREE

THE tree that gives milk is one of the most famous phenomena of nature. It is found most frequently along the northern Cordillera of South America, and is called by the natives "the milk tree" (arbol de leche).

Humboldt made a special study of this tree. Let him tell it:

"We can scarcely conceive how the human race could exist without farinaceous substances, and without that nourishing juice which the breast of the mother contains. The amylaceous matter of corn, the object of religious veneration among so many nations, ancient and modern, is diffused in the seeds, and deposited in the roots of vegetables; milk, which serves as an aliment, appears to us exclusively the produce of animal organization. Such are the impressions we have received in our earliest infancy: such is also the source of that astonishment created by the aspect of the cow tree. A few drops of vegetable juice recall to our mind all the powerfulness and fecundity of nature. On the barren flank of a rock grows a tree with coriaceous and dry leaves. Its large woody roots can scarcely penetrate into the stone. For several months of the year not a single shower moistens its foliage. Its branches appear dead and dried; but when the trunk is pierced there flows from it a sweet and nourishing milk. It is at the rising of the sun that this vegetable fountain is most abundant. The negroes and natives are then seen hastening from all quarters, furnished with large bowls to receive the milk, which grows yellow and thickens at the surface. Some empty their bowls under the tree itself, others carry the juice home to their children.

"In examining the physical properties of animal and vegetable products, science displays them as closely linked together. Nothing appears isolated; the chemical principles that were found to be peculiar to animals are found in plants; a common chain links together all organic nature."

THE WINGLESS BIRD

PERHAPS the very strangest and most weird of all living birds is the *apteryx*, or Kiwi-kiwi. This bird has scarcely the slightest trace of wings, a peculiarity which has gained for it the name of Apteryx, or "wingless." The common cognomen "Kiwi-kiwi" is adapted from its peculiar repetitious call.

This singular bird is a native of New Zealand, where it was once very common, but is slowly becoming extinct, a fate from which it has been hitherto preserved by its nocturnal and retiring habits. The bird lives mostly among the ferns and always remains concealed during the day. It is remarkably fleet of foot, diving among the leaves with singular adroitness. It feeds upon insects of various kinds, particularly worms which it attracts to the surface by striking on the ground with its powerful feet.

The kiwi-kiwi is a little larger than an ordinary domestic fowl.

THERE ARE MORE THAN 4,000 DIFFERENT WAYS OF SPELLING THE NAME SHAKESPEARE

MOST of the literary people who believe that Bacon is Shakespeare—and they are many—also maintain that the Stratfordian was so uneducated that he could not write so much as his own name!

There are only five pieces of writing in the world that may be supposed to have been written by Shakespeare's pen, and if these be authentic then it is certain that the famous bard has spelled his own name in several different ways. In his own Will, he has written it "I William Shackspeare." Another time he writes it "Shakspeare." And again "Wilm Shaxpr."

Evidently there is no authentic way of spelling the name so I append a few of the 4,000 different ways.

SHAKESPEARE	SHAXPUR	SHAKESPEYRE
SHAKSPARE	SHAXKSPERE	SHAXSPERE
SCHAKESPERE	SHAKSPEYR	SAXSPEAR
SCHAKSPEARE	SHAXPEARE	SCHACKSPERE
SHAKESPEAR	SAXPERE	SAXPEARE
CHACSPER	SHAKESPER	SCHAKESPEIRE
SHAXPERE	SHACKSPER	SCHAKSPERE

SHACKSPEARE	SHAXSPEARE	SHAKSPER
SHAXKSPERE	SHACKESPUR	SCHACKSPUR
SHAXPUR	SHAXXPEARE	SHAXEPER
SHAXSPER	SHACKESPEIR	SHAXPER
SHAKESPERE	SCHAXESPER	SAXSPERE
SHAXKESPERE	SCHAXSPEIR	SHACKSPUR
SHAGSPERE	SCHAXESPEARE	CHACSPEAR
SHAXSPERE	SAXESPEYRE	SHAKESPAIRE
SHACKSPIRE	CHACKESPEARE	SHAXPEYRE
SHAKEYSPEERE	SAXPEARE	SHAKSPEARE
SHAKESPEYRE	SHAXESPUR	SHAKESPEIRE
SHAKESPEARE	SHAKSPERE	SCHAXESPEAR
SHAKSPEYR	SHAKESPEER	SCHAXSPEARE
SHACSPERE	SHAXPERE	SHACHESPEAR
SHAKYSPER	SHAKESPEYR	SAXSPEARE
SHACESPEARE	SHACKSPERE	SHAXESPEIRE
SHAXESPUR	SHACKESPEYRE	SCHAXPEIRE
SHAXKESPEYR	SHAKISPERE	Etc.

The full list can be found in "A Plea for Reformed Spelling," by Alexander John Ellis.

A FRENCH BIPLANE
FLIES WITHOUT A PILOT
IT TAKES OFF AND
LANDS UNDER
WIRELESS CONTROL

NATURE'S MARKSMAN
—THE BEAKED CHÆTODON FISH — of India
USES ITS ELONGATED MUZZLE AS A GUN TO SHOOT INSECTS
—USING DROPS OF WATER AS BULLETS !

$$2^{117}-1$$

170,141,183,460,469,229,731,687,303,715,884,105,727
— IS THE LARGEST NUMBER THAT CANNOT BE DIVIDED BY ANY OTHER
Discovered by LUCAS IN 1877.

MRS. MATHILDE KOVACS
BURNED UP 500,000,000 KRONEN
TO SPITE HER HEIRS — on the day before her death. 1917.

MISS
JOYCE
WETHERED
MADE 2 BIRDIES
ON ONE HOLE
(HER DRIVE HIT A
SWALLOW — AND SHE
GOT A 4.)

NATURE'S MARKSMAN

THE Beaked Chaetodon, the fish of heavenly hues that goes hunting with a gun, is found in the mouths of rivers emptying into the East Indian and Polynesian Seas.

The curiously elongated muzzle is used by this fish as a gun with which it shoots drops of water. If it sees a fly or another insect resting on a twig or grass-blade overhanging the water, the Chaetodon approaches very quietly, the greater part of its body submerged, and its long nose just showing above the surface with its point aimed at the victim. Suddenly, it shoots a drop of water at the unsuspecting insect with such accuracy that it is knocked off its perch into the water where it is instantly snapped up.

This habit it continues even in captivity, and is in consequence in great estimation as a household pet in Japan. The Japanese keep the fish in a large bowl of water, and amuse themselves by holding towards it a fly upon the end of a slender rod and watching the finny marksman shoot its prey into the water.

* * *

GOLF BIRDIES

Scoring birdies at golf is a worthy achievement anytime, but to get two birdies on one hole is indeed a rarity.

Miss Joyce Wethered, who is probably the greatest woman golfer the game has yet produced, accomplished this feat in a practice game last year (1927). Her drive struck a swallow that flew over the fairway, but despite this accident, Miss Wethered was successful in breaking par for the hole.

Miss Wethered held the women's golf championship at the same time that her brother, Roger Wethered, held the British amateur championship.

* * *

BURNING ANGER

BECAUSE her relatives were discourteous to her pet cats, Mrs. Mathilde Kovacs revenged herself by burning up her fortune just before her death. This bit of spite work was reported extensively in the Vienna newspapers during March, 1917.

FIGURES DON'T LIE

NUMBERS have a magic lure and there is no end to the marvels that can be performed by one who is proficient. Figures may never lie but they can make you think that they do. The potency of numbers is alarming. The enormous totals reached by geometrical progressions and ordinary transpositions is almost beyond comprehension.

THE
MAGIC BLOCKS
—
ALL THE PEOPLE
ON EARTH –
WORKING DAY AND NIGHT
– FOR A MILLION YEARS
COULD NOT
ARRANGE 5 LETTER-BLOCKS
INTO ALL POSSIBLE COMBINATIONS

Five letter-blocks contain a total of 30 letters. There are 620,448,401,-735,259,439,369,000 different transpositions possible with 30 letters. At the rate of one transposition a second, it would take one man 1,967,428,975,-879,120 years to arrange the blocks into all the possible combinations.

If all the 1,800,000,000 people on earth helped him it would still require 1,093,016 years to do it.

* * *

An old story that will give you an idea of the startling fecundity of figures is that one about the boy who innocently offered to go to work for one cent the first day if his employer would double his salary each day for a month. The employer innocently agreed, and dropped dead when he learned that on the last day of the month the salary of his office boy would amount to $5,368,709.12 for that day alone, and a total of $10,737,418.23 for the month.

$1 \times 91 = 091$
$2 \times 91 = 182$
$3 \times 91 = 273$
$4 \times 91 = 364$
$5 \times 91 = 455$
$6 \times 91 = 546$
$7 \times 91 = 637$
$8 \times 91 = 728$
$9 \times 91 = 819$

* * *

$3 \times 37 = 111$
$6 \times 37 = 222$
$9 \times 37 = 333$
$12 \times 37 = 444$
$15 \times 37 = 555$
$18 \times 37 = 666$
$21 \times 37 = 777$
$24 \times 37 = 888$
$27 \times 37 = 999$

* * *

$33 \times 3367 = 111111$
$66 \times 3367 = 222222$
$99 \times 3367 = 333333$
$132 \times 3367 = 444444$
$165 \times 3367 = 555555$
$198 \times 3367 = 666666$
$231 \times 3367 = 777777$
$264 \times 3367 = 888888$
$297 \times 3367 = 999999$

* * *

$123456789 \times 9 = 1111111111$
$123456789 \times 18 = 2222222222$
$123456789 \times 27 = 3333333333$
Etc.

111

CAN YOU WRITE THE ANSWER?

$$9(9^9) = ?$$

The above figure expresses 9 raised to the 9th power of 9, or 9 raised to the 387,420,489th power. It is the largest sum that can be indicated by 3 figures.

The final answer will contain 369 millions of digits. Allowing for 5 digits to the inch, the length of tape required to write down the answer would be 1,164 miles, and the ordinary human span of life would be sadly insufficient to accomplish the task.

Ref.: "Mathematische Mussestunden," by Dr. Herman Schubert.

* * *

MAGIC SEVEN

SEVEN is the holy number. There are 7 days in creation, 7 days in the week, 7 phases of the moon, every 7th year was sabbatical, and 7 times 7 years was the jubilee. There are 7 ages in the life of man, 7 divisions in the Lord's Prayer, 7 bibles, 7 churches of Asia, 7 Graces, 7 Deadly Sins, 7 Senses, 7 Sorrows of the Virgin, 7 Virtues, 7 Joys of the Virgin, 7 Precious Things of the Buddhas, 7 Sleepers of Ephesus, 7 Lamps of Architecture. The apostles chose 7 deacons, Enoch, who was translated, was 7th from Adam; Jesus Christ was the 77th in a direct line. Our Lord spoke 7 times on the cross, on which He was 7 hours; He appeared 7 times; and after 7 times 7 days He sent the Holy Ghost. There appeared 7 golden candlesticks and 7 stars in the hand of Him that was in the midst; 7 lambs before the 7 spirits of God; the book with the 7 seals; the lamb with 7 horns and 7 eyes; 7 angels bearing 7 plagues, and 7 vials of wrath. The vision of Daniel was 70 weeks; and the elders of Israel were 70. There were also 7 heavens, 7 planets, 7 stars, 7 wise men, 7 champions of Christendom, 7 notes in music, 7 primary colors, 7 sacraments of the Catholic Church, and 7 wonders of the world. The 7th son was considered endowed with pre-eminent wisdom; and the 7th son of a 7th son is still thought to possess the power of healing diseases spontaneously.

And the opposite sides of the dice total 7.

CAN YOU CHANGE FIVE DOLLARS!

"Certainly!" you will say.

But you can't do it!

If you changed a five-dollar bill into all the different ways possible—cents, nickels, dimes, quarters, halves, and dollars—it would require exactly 2,305,-843,009,213,693,951 different changes; and if you made a change each second —day and night—it would take you 103 years to do it!

* * *

142857

The mystic number. All the figures appear in the sum when multiplied as follows:

$$142857 \times 2 = 285714$$
$$142857 \times 3 = 428571$$
$$142857 \times 4 = 571428$$
$$142857 \times 5 = 714285$$
$$142857 \times 6 = 857142$$

and then

$$142857 \times 7 = 999999$$

* * *

PALINDROMATIC FIGURES

$$11^2 = 121$$
$$111^2 = 12321$$
$$1111^2 = 1234321$$
$$11111^2 = 123454321$$

Etc.

* * *

The following legend is told in connection with the invention of the game of chess. An East Indian Potentate was so pleased with the game that he promised the inventor, a slave, the fulfillment of any wish. The slave asked for the number of grains of wheat which would result, if one grain were placed on the first square of the chess-board, two on the second, four on the third, etc., i.e., each time twice as many as on the last. At first glance, this wish seemed to be a modest one, but calculations showed that it would be impossible for the king to keep his promise, even if he owned the whole earth and spent his entire life growing wheat on it. The result is: 18 quintillions, 446 quadrillions, 744 trillions, 73 billions, 709 millions, 551,615 grains.

THE 100 SYMBOLS

All the books ever written in all the libraries of the world containing all the wit, wisdom, poetry, fiction, history and scientific knowledge ever offered to humanity—or ever apt to be offered in the future—are expressed in letters.

It is all done with about 100 symbols. By symbols I mean the ordinary letters of the alphabet—both cases, figures, interpunctions, and mathematical signs. The number of symbols is limited, and of course the number of possible transpositions of these 100 symbols is limited.

Since the number of transpositions of 100 symbols is limited the printed word must be limited and therefore all literature imaginable must be rendered in a limited number of volumes.

Assume that it is possible to write exhaustively about a subject in a volume of the size of "Believe It or Not." Assume that 1,000,000 transpositions of symbols are used in printing this book. By combining to the limits of possibility the 100 symbols in lots of 1,000,000 we can determine the number of volumes ever written or ever likely to be written in the future.

With 1,000,000 symbols to a volume, you will have as many volumes as will equal the original number of symbols 100 raised to the 1,000,000th power. The answer will contain a figure with 2,000,000 noughts after it, and would require a strip of paper 2 miles long to write it out in type the size of this. If the books were each one inch thick and placed side by side the number of inches would equal the number of books—in other words this shelf of books would be as many inches long as indicated by a figure of 2,000,0001 digits. Reduced to miles, it would be as many miles long as a figure of 1,999,996 digits.

Suppose you want a book at the opposite end of this book shelf, you would have to travel as fast as light if you ever got there in any comprehensible length of time. If you traveled as fast as light—180,000 miles a second—you would travel 6 quadrillion miles in a year, and to reach the book at the end of the line will take as many years as the figure 6,000,-000,000,000,000 is contained in the figure of the distance—or as many years as are to be expressed in a figure written with 1,999,980 noughts. It is beyond human conception.

And the book would probably be gone when you got there.

Raimundus Lullus, Giordano Bruno, Kurt Lasswitz, Leibnitz, and others devoted lifetimes to these calculations.

$$1\times9+2=11$$
$$12\times9+3=111$$
$$123\times9+4=1111$$
$$1234\times9+5=11111$$
$$12345\times9+6=111111$$
$$123456\times9+7=1111111$$
$$1234567\times9+8=11111111$$
$$12345678\times9+9=111111111$$
$$123456789\times9+10=1111111111$$
$$1\times8+1=9$$
$$12\times8+2=98$$
$$123\times8+3=987$$
$$1234\times8+4=9876$$
$$12345\times8+5=98765$$
$$123456\times8+6=987654$$
$$1234567\times8+7=9876543$$
$$12345678\times8+8=98765432$$
$$123456789\times8+9=987654321$$
$$65359477124183\times17\times1=1111111111111111$$
$$65359477124183\times17\times2=2222222222222222$$
$$65359477124183\times17\times3=3333333333333333$$
$$65359477124183\times17\times4=4444444444444444$$
$$65359477124183\times17\times5=5555555555555555$$

Etc.

* * *

THE PERSISTENT NUMBER

526,315,789,473,684,210

You may multiply the above figure with any number you choose and the original figures will always reappear in the result.

* * *

THE LARGEST PRIME KNOWN

170,141,183,460,469,231,731,687,303,715,864,105,727

This figure is the largest known number that cannot be divided by any other. It was discovered by Arthur Lucas in 1877. It is $2^{127}-1$.

MAGIC SQUARES

These numbers—as per number of squares in the diagrams—are so placed that all columns add the same, horizontally, vertically, and diagonally.

15

6	1	8
7	5	3
2	9	4

34

1	14	15	4
8	11	10	5
12	7	6	9
13	2	3	16

"PI"

The letter Π (pi) indicates the incommensurable relationship between the diameter of any circle and its circumference. The number is usually given as 3.14159+. Here is the value worked out to 707 decimal places. The figures are not to be found in many places and they may be desired as a curiosity by some amateur mathematicians:

3.14159	26535	89793	23846	26433	83279	50288	41971
69399	37510	58209	74944	59230	78164	06286	20899
86280	34825	34211	70679	82148	08651	32823	06647
09384	46095	50582	23172	53594	08128	48111	74502
84102	70193	85211	05559	64462	29489	54930	38196
44288	10675	66593	34461	28475	64823	27867	83165
27120	19091	45648	56692	34603	48610	49432	66482
13393	60226	02491	41273	72458	70066	06315	58817
48815	20920	96282	92540	91715	36436	78925	90360
01133	05354	88204	66521	38414	69519	41511	60943
30572	70365	75959	19530	92186	11738	19326	11793
10511	85480	74462	38798	34749	56735	18857	52724
89122	79381	83011	94912	98336	73362	44193	66430
86021	39501	60924	48077	23094	36285	53096	62027
55693	97986	95022	24749	96206	07497	03041	23669
86199	51100	89202	38377	02131	41694	11902	98858
25446	81639	79990	46597	00081	70029	63123	77381
34208	41307	91451	18398	05709	85+.		

*   *   *

ONE PROBLEM NEVER PROVED

Mathematicians have been able to prove most of the problems submitted to them, but there is one for which no mathematical proof has even been devised, and that is why a mapmaker need use but four colors to print his maps. The fact has been known for centuries, but no one has ever determined a method by which it could be proved. If you try drawing you will soon find that it is impossible to draw any figure of five districts each of which touches the other four, the only circumstance under which more than four colors would be necessary to mark the divisions.

KASPAR HAUSER COULD SEE THE STARS
IN THE DAY TIME

KASPAR HAUSER, the mystery child of Europe who has been written about so often by authors of the past and present, could see the stars shining at noon without mechanical aid. The stars never really disappear you know, and the eyes of this famous boy were abnormal.

Kaspar Hauser was said to be the Heir to the throne of the Grandduchy of Baden. He was abducted in infancy and placed in solitary confinement in a dark room for 18 years. He first saw the light of day when he wandered from his cell and apparently appeared from nowhere in Anspach, Bavaria. Although he was nearly a grown man, his mental development was that of a two-year-old child. The mystery surrounding him, and his curious behavior, aroused a great deal of interest at the time . . . and since.

118

BABE RUTH HIT 125 HOME RUNS IN ONE HOUR

RUTH, greatest of all baseball players, performed this prodigious clouting feat in an exhibition game on Wrigley Field, Los Angeles, February, 1927. Babe, who always aims to please, stood at the plate for an hour while several pitchers tossed balls at him which he walloped over the fence—125 in all.

119

THE HANDY LETTER WRITER

HERR KURTZ received an anonymous letter daily for twenty years! He is the owner of one of the Government tobacconist's stores of Vienna in the 2nd ward, and after a few years of receiving the letter he tried to induce the Minister of Post and Telegraphs of Austria to refrain from delivering his mail altogether but his efforts were unsuccessful. The letters arrived daily from 1901 to 1921 and then ceased suddenly as though the tireless sender had died at last.

Curiously enough the contents of the letter were entirely innocent.

Ref.: "Neue Freie Presse" of Feb. 1921.

* * *

THE BOOK WORM

GUSTAVE LEBAIR, who, for 60 years read the same book daily at the Bibliothèque Nationale, was a famous bibliomaniac and well known to frequenters of the Bibliothèque Nationale of Paris. The particular book he read, "St. Appolonius of Tiane," was in some way connected with an event in his youth.

The book *"Bibliomania"* by Hertzen, where I found the statement about Lebair, goes to some lengths to explain his persistence on psychological grounds. Bibliomaniacs are book lovers whose passion manifests itself in some strange way.

* * *

A BEAVER'S DAM

François I, King of France, issued a decree making the wearing of whiskers punishable by death.

"Qu'ils aient dedans 3 jours a faire ou oster leur dite Barbe
sous peine de la hart."

Receuils des Ordinances Folio 48 Paris, 1557.

"THE PLACE OF DRUNKENNESS"

THE Indian word for New York is Manhattan, or Manna-ha-ta, and means "The Place of Drunkenness." This name is traceable to the year 1524 when Giovanni Verrazzano, the Florentine explorer, landed for the first time at what is now the lower extremity of New York City and gave the Indians their first taste of firewater. A good time was had by all, and ever after the natives referred to the island as "Manna-ha-ta" or "place of drunkenness."
Ref.: Rev. John Gottlieb E. Heckewelder's "History of Early Manhattan."

* * *

THE IDEAL LANDLORD

Frau C. Worth, owner of a large apartment house in Berlin, did not collect any rents from her tenants for twenty years.

* * *

A WEEK WITH TWO THURSDAYS

ON AN occasion in 1147, Pope Eugene III reached Paris on a Friday. Inasmuch as Friday was a fast day, and to enable the populace properly to celebrate his entry into the city, the Pope decreed that Friday was Thursday! Hence a week with two Thursdays.

* * *

ENDURING FAME

"Chauffeurs" were a famous band of brigands in France in 1793. They were so called because they tortured their victims by burning their feet.

* * *

The following is a news item from the Barstow (Cal.) *Times*. It reads:
"Bill Jarrett has just returned to Barstow from the Death Valley country. Bill worked for six weeks on the graveyard shift for the Corpse Mining Company in the Coffin mine, located in Dead Man's Canyon in Funeral Range at the end of Death Valley. Bill is leaving next week for a prospecting trip to the Devil's Playground in Hell's Half Acre."

* * *

THE BOBBING ISLAND

IN LAKE ILFUNGEN, in Livonia, is a small island that does a disappearing act once each year. Toward the end of October, or early in November, the island sinks beneath the surface of the lake.

In the spring the island reappears and remains all summer, so that farmers raise and cut hay on it.

121

SIDIS
—THE PRODIGY
COULD RECITE
THE ALPHABET
AT THE AGE OF
6 MONTHS

THE FIG-TREE TOMB
BEN WANGFORD - AN ENGLISH NAVAL OFFICER (1800)
WAS BURIED WITH A FIG IN HIS HAND (– his dying wish)
AND THE TREE HAS BURST THE TOMB !
PARISH CHURCH, WATFORD, ENG.

W.C. PERRY
of Belleville, Kan.
MADE A HOLE-IN-ONE
ON A BLIND
HOLE
June
1928

THE PEG-LEGGED COW

THE FIG-TREE TOMB

THIS celebrated curiosity can be seen in a little churchyard a few miles outside of London. It is located close beside the Parish Church (St. Mary) in Watford, an ancient shrine of faith where "Prayer and Praise have been offered to God for seven hundred years."

The Rev. Henry Edwards, Vicar, sent me the following information about the man who was buried with a fig in his hand. The Vicar concluded with a prayer.

> "The Fig-Tree Tomb, near the S. wall of the Parish Church of Watford, is the source of many old tales, the most authentic being that of Ben Wangford, a naval officer, who did not believe in the future life, and wished when buried to have something placed with his remains that might germinate and burst the tomb, in order that, if it did, his friends would know that his opinion was wrong.

*   *   *

SIDIS—THE PRODIGY

SIDIS was one of the four noted American prodigies; Winifred Stoner II, Edward Harvey, Jr., and John Trumbull, the poet, were the other three.

Dr. Boris Sidis, professor at Harvard, was his father.

At the age of six months Sidis could recite the alphabet; at two he could read and write; and at the age of eleven he matriculated in Harvard and astounded his professors by discussing the fourth dimension.

*   *   *

THE ILLITERATE CALCULATOR

Jedediah Buxton, the illiterate calculator, in a month's time, without the aid of paper or pencil, figured out that a cubical mile could contain 586,040,972,673,024,000 human hairs. It took him three months to multiply an English farthing 140 times with itself, arriving at the figure of 725,958,-238,096,074,907,868,531,656,993,638,851,106 Pounds, 2 Shillings, 8 pence.

He was then asked to multiply this stupendous sum by itself and after two and one-half months announced the result to be 527,015,363,459,557,-385, 673, 733,542,638,591,721,213,298,966,079,307,524,904,381,389,499,251,-637,423,236 pounds.

THE GIRAFFE GIRL

"—On the road to Mandalay,
Where the flyin'-fishes play,
An' the dawn comes up like thunder
outer China 'crost the Bay!"

IF you follow the above road to Toungoo and then ascend the hills to the west you will come to the land of the Giraffe women, the long-necked Burmese belles of Padaung. The Kewawngdu, as they call themselves, are remarkable for the extraordinary collars of brass that they weld around their necks from time to time until a giraffe-like effect is obtained.

In Burma "Her throat is like the swan" is not a mere poetic figure of speech in so far as length is concerned. Some of the women brought down to Mandalay to be gazed at by the Great King of Righteousness and the Dwellers in the Palace, have necks fourteen and fifteen inches long.

The neckband consists of brass rods, as thick as your little finger, commencing with a wide base on the shoulder blades and reaching up to the chin. Little girls begin wearing them as early as possible usually starting with five rings, which are as much as most of them can manage, but as the neck is kept constantly on the stretch, additional ones are added from time to time until the ordinary limit of twenty-one coils is reached. Twenty-five and more have been worn, however.

At the back of the neck, fastened through the main coil, is a large heavy ring which is used for tying up these rubber-necked ladies whenever the occasion demands such procedure.

If the family be well-to-do, similar coils of brass are added to the arms and legs; and the length of these seems only limited by the ability to pay for the rings—for brass is very expensive. Sometimes the total weight of brass carried by Padaung flappers is as much as sixty or seventy pounds: yet burdened with this weight, they hoe the fields, carry water for domestic use, and brew liquor.

The brass-collar fashion has no apparent effect on their health, and the only noticeable effect is that the women speak as if someone had them tight around the neck.

A KEWAWNGDU

GOD'S HEAVEN

OF COURSE you expect to go to Heaven when you die. We all do. The hope is in all of us, that when we die, we will go to Heaven and rejoin the other members of our family who have passed on.

Take my advice: make a reservation. Heaven is becoming very crowded and it is extremely doubtful whether you can get in; and should you manage to squeeze yourself past the pearly gates it is even more doubtful whether you could find your family among all that crowd.

We will say that you go to Heaven to meet your father and mother and the rest of your kith and kin. When you meet your father and mother, they will be with their father and mother, for they would have the same desire to be with their parents as you have to be with them. And their parents in turn would be with their parents; so on back through the countless generations of mankind.

So you will have to meet them all. You cannot be snooty in Heaven, you know, and snub anybody.

Now, if we take 25 years as a generation, we find that there have been 77 generations since the time of Christ. And if we count only your parents, their parents, and so on backward for that length of time, we find that you will have to meet 302,231,454,903,657,293,676,543 different relatives.

Our own little world would not hold that stupendous number.

If that many people were on earth today they would have to be stacked up on each others' heads. Allowing them two feet to stand on this would make a stack of one solid mass of folks 113,236 miles high all over the earth's surface.

Suppose you wanted to say "hello" to your dear old grandfather who happened to be located some 113,000 miles up the heap. Of course you would have to climb—there would be no other way except to scramble up this human bean-stalk like little Jack. Let us assume that you can climb one-half as fast as the U. S. Army marches—which is 15 miles a day. If you climbed at the rate of 8 miles a day you would reach your old grandpap about 39 years later —providing you didn't get yourself knocked off meanwhile for stepping on somebody's ear in the ascent. Of course you will be able to slide down faster and should reach your own place in Heaven about 50 years after you left it.

That is 2 generations— which means that maybe your children and some of your children's children will have squeezed in and been looking around for you. You really couldn't expect anybody to hold your place for you for 50 years, so do not be surprised if you are out all around and not able to find your own children anywhere . . . which means that you will have a hell of a time in Heaven.

Mind you, the above figures do not include brothers, sisters, uncles, aunts, nieces, nephews, cousins and other relatives. Also I am allowing only for 1928 years, although scientists tell us that man has been on earth for countless generations before that time—some estimate it as 100,000 years. And, since science has proved so conclusively that you are related to all animals with four legs or a long tail that have lived on this earth for the last 100,000,000 years, you will have to include them too. They are all your ancestors!

As a social proposition the celestial outlook appears a bit embarrassing, doesn't it?

St. John records the limits of Heaven in Revelations, XXI., 16:

". . . He measured the city with the reed, twelve thousand furlongs. The length, and the breadth, and the height of it are equal."

Twelve thousand furlongs is 7,920,000 feet, and when cubed this is equal to 496,793,088,000,000,000,000 cubic feet—in other words Heaven as visualized by St. John is about 15 miles long in each dimension. If you allow 10 cubic feet as ample space for a human being, you will find that Heaven can hold about 49,679,308,800,000,000,000 persons if packed in tight. This calculation does not allow for the streets of gold or the trees of marvelous leaves and fruits, or the "pure river of water of life, clear as crystal, proceeding out of the throne of God and of the Lamb."

It is apparent that Heaven was filled up several hundred years ago—or about the time that Columbus was discovering America.

What to do?

Obviously there is but one way out. You must die sometime, and since it is so evident that you cannot go to Heaven, where shall you go——?

You said it.

THE VOCAL MEMNON

The Statue That Speaks

A MILE from the Nile on the opposite shore from the ruins of Karnak two huge stone figures sit in staring isolation. Each represents a colossal king 64 feet high, seated upon a throne, which is itself supported by a pedestal. Though the faces of both have been hacked out of all human resemblance, everyone knows that these statues are the effigies of the same King —Amunoph, or Amenhotep, whose son's daughter married King Tut.

One of the colossi is mute, but the other is the famous Vocal Memnon, the statue that speaks!

That is—it did speak. There are 87 legible Greek and Latin inscriptions upon the legs of Memnon which testify to the time and hour of the day at which the phenomenon was heard. Famous men of many ages listened. There are the words of Emperor Hadrian, Sabina, his wife, Tacitus, Pliny, Pausanias, Lucian, and Strabo describing the miraculous musical sound emanating from the stone . . . "like the snapping of a huge harp string" . . . "like the sound of smitten brass." Some heard the voice of the image several times. According to the inscriptions February and March seemed to be by far the most propitious months, and the morning hour the most favored vocally—as soon indeed as the sun's rays fell upon the statue—as though "Aurora kissing her son upon the lips received an articulate reply."

The explanation?

Two alone of the many hypotheses put forward are worth considering. A multitude of wild conjectures, based principally on imagination, but claiming pseudo-scientific or mechanical interest, crumble away when touched by the merciless finger of fact. There remain the rival theories that the voice of Memnon was a fraud practised by the ancient Egyptian priests; and the other that it was a natural phenomenon to be explained by physical causes. The latter theory has the most credence—the conclusion irresistibly suggests itself that the sound was due to some peculiar relation between the warmth of the rising sun and the great block of cracked and sundered stone.

It has been a long time since our hero has spoken, and it seems that

Memnon's lyre has lost the chord
That breathed the mystic tone.

Certainly they do not recognize the cartoonist's profession. I was stared at in stony silence on the occasion that I stood before the Vocal Memnon and his mute companion and waited patiently for a word from them. It was near dusk, and the glowing sun was sinking suddenly down behind the hills that enclose the Valley of the Tombs of the Kings as it caused the images to darken hugely and throw out long-streaking shadows that emphasized the size of them and made their silence louder than words.

THE KING WHO WAS CROWNED
BEFORE HE WAS BORN

Apparently such a thing could never happen.

But it did.

In Persia, during the 4th century, the wife of Shah Hormouz remained pregnant at the time of her husband's death, and the uncertainty of the sex of the unborn child, as well as the event, excited the ambitious hopes of the princes of the house of Sassan who were moved to seize the throne.

The apprehensions of civil war were at length removed by the positive assurances of the Magi that the widow of Hormouz had conceived and would safely produce a son. Obedient to the voice of superstition, the Persians prepared, without delay, the ceremony of his coronation. A royal bed on which the Queen lay in state was exhibited in the midst of the palace in the presence of the assembled multitude, and the crown of the Sassanids was placed on the spot which might be supposed to conceal the future heir. Meanwhile the prostrated assembly adored the invisible and insensible sovereign.

The magi proved to be correct in their prophecies, and the crowned child was a boy who lived to rule an extraordinary length of time under the name of Sapor II.

Ref.: Gibbon's "Decline and Fall."

* * *

Chou Kung, who invented the compass, had a swivel wrist on which he could turn his hand completely around.

* * *

Lollia Paulina, wife of Caesar Caligula, wore a dress valued at $2,000,000 and a pearl necklace worth $3,500,000.

Ref.: Pliny the Elder.

* * *

A small toy balloon was released in New Jersey by A. Perry and was found later in Venezuela by J. Quintero of Maracaibo.

* * *

Leon Avazian, of New York, climbed the stairs to the top of the Woolworth Building in 9 minutes. 55 stories. 1520 steps.

THE 153-YEAR-OLD BRIDEGROOM

Zaro Agha is never too old to yearn.

The stalwart old Turk, who is probably the oldest person alive, was married in 1927 despite his 153 years. During his long and eventful life, Agha has buried ten wives and twenty-seven children, but he was not discouraged and his spirit is ever young—and the mystery of a woman's veil allured him.

Zaro possesses a keen memory which enables him to tell tales of events that reach back to our Revolutionary War days. He makes an annual visit to President Kemal who always gives him a hearty handshake and several hundred liras. The Governor of the city of Constantinople has presented him with a house, and last year the Prefect made him Municipal Doorkeeper for life.

THE EYELESS INFANT

THIS child is now four years old and normal in every way except for the complete absence of eyes. He was born with his frontal bone joining to the cheek bones which eliminated even the eye sockets which are but slightly indicated by two small depressions.

The boy was born in Sablonceaux (Charente Inférieure), France, and has six brothers and sisters who are all normal.

Ref.: Gazette Medicale de Paris.

*   *   *

Robert Jones who performs this remarkable feat of strength and balance is worthy of a place among the famous Joneses of athletic history. Young Robert is a pupil of the celebrated Paulinetti, and is an accomplished acrobat and gymnast.

He stands on his thumbs on Indian clubs with ease—and he is ready to do it anytime.

Jones lives in Philadelphia where he is attached to the editorial staff of the *Strength Magazine*.

*   *   *

THE LYRE BIRD

THIS beautiful bird is obviously so-called from the shape of its tail. The extraordinary tail of this bird is often upwards of two feet in length, and consists of sixteen feathers, formed and arranged in a very graceful and curious manner. The two outer feathers are broadly webbed, and, as may be seen, in the illustration, are curved in a manner that produces the appearance of an ancient lyre. The two central tail-feathers are narrowly webbed, and all the others are modified with long slender shafts, bearded with alternate feathery filaments which well represent the strings of the lyre.

The tail is seen in its greatest beauty between the months of June and September after which time it is shed. The bird is a native of New South Wales.

THE
EYELESS
INFANT
— of SABLONCEAUX (Charente- Inferieure, France)
WAS BORN
WITHOUT ANY
EYES. WHATEVER.
1925

ROBERT
JONES
— of Pine Bluff, Ark.
CAN STAND ON
HIS THUMBS
ON INDIAN CLUBS

PHIL HANNA
— of Epworth, Ill.
HAS HANGED
55 CRIMINALS

THE
LYRE
BIRD

133

SINGING SANDS

ONE warm afternoon in Honolulu—it seems to be always afternoon there
—I was stretched full length on the sands of Waikiki doing nothing—
as is my wont—except watching the two Kahanomoku boys and Kealoha do
tricks on their surf boards when the Duke casually suggested "Why don't
you draw a picture of the Barking Sands?"

What?

"Sure," continued the Duke, "the sands of Kauai over yonder actually bark
when you step on them."

Sands that bark, eh? I had to see the doggone place. Kauai is one of the
western islands of the Hawaiian group about 75 miles from Honolulu. Along
the shore at Nahili is this series of wind-blown sand-hills about 60 feet high
and stretching along for about a half mile. The front wall is quite steep. The
bright white sand is composed of coral, shells and particles of lava, and true
enough it possessed the particular property of emitting a sound, when stepped
on, like the barking of a dog. Two handsful when clapped together produce
the same phenomenon. The sound varies with the degree of heat, the dryness
of the sand, and the amount of friction employed. The drier the sand the
louder the sound—and our running foot steps sounded like rolling thunder.

Since then I have learned that this strange caper of nature is known in
other parts of the world under different names such as Singing Sands, Sound-
ing Sands, Rumbling Sands, Musical Sands, etc.

Marco Polo wrote of the musical sand-hills of Tunyang in Central Asia.
Ibn Batutah, the Moor of Tangier, speaks of the Hill of Drums near Mecca.
The famous Friar Odoric tells of the Reg-i-Ruwan, or Moving Sands of
Kabul, and Lord Curzon writes of many of them in his "Tales of Travel."

The exact cause of this sonorous quality in sand has not been fully agreed
upon. The scientific explanation is rather difficult. The American researchers,
Doctors Bolton and Julien arrived at the following conclusion:

"The true cause of the sonorous property is connected with thin
pellicles or films of air or of gases thence derived, deposited, and condensed upon the surface of the sand-grains during gradual evapora-
tion, after wetting by the sea, lakes or rains. By virtue of these films
the sand-grains become separated by elastic cushions of condensed
gases, capable of considerable vibration. The extent of the vibration

and the amount and tone of the sound thereby produced after quick disturbance of the sand, is largely dependent upon the forms, structures, and surfaces of the sand-grains, and especially upon their purity or freedom from fine silt or dust."

OYSTERS THAT CATCH MICE

IRISH oysters of course! Probably bi-valves of any other nationality would not be so pugnacious.

Be that as it may, there has been a battle royal going on this year on the northeast coast islands off Donegal. Thus far the limpets have had far the better of it and thousands of rats have fallen in the unequal struggle.

The armies of rats which infest this district have been adventuring to the waterside in quest of food. At low tide the rats insert their noses between the partly opened shells of the oysters, hoping to make a meal off the edible shell-fish, but the latter are exceedingly sensitive to the slightest touch and instantly close on their enemies with a vise-like grip. The rats are held tight as in traps, and soon the rising tide creeps in and crowns the oysters victors.

* * *

Here is a letter from Mr. Henry C. Avery, of Fishers Island, New York.

"Dear Rip:

Yesterday at low tide my family and I were witnesses to a tragedy of unusual nature. A pair of kingfishers had been our friends for weeks, making our dock their headquarters, and flying around us without fear.

My daughter and I were digging clams in about an inch of water, when one of the kingfishers darted down within a few feet of us and struck at something in the water. He struggled with it as a robin often does with a worm. The struggle lasted not more than half a minute as we walked toward the bird. As I drew near the bird was still. I tried to lift it from the water but it held fast. I then dug deep into the mud and brought up a large clam of the hard-shell variety which had clamped firmly to the bird's bill. The bird was dead, either drowned or died of fright.

Believe It or Not,
Henry C. Avery.
Aug. 7, 1925."

A Billion Dollars in London is Worth a Thousand Times As Much As a Billion Dollars in New York

Strange as it may seem, an English billionaire is many times richer than an American billionaire.

And why not?

A billion in England is a million million (1,000,000,000,000), but in the United States a billion is considered to be a thousand million (1,000,000,000). See any dictionary.

* * *

A SPIDER IS NOT AN INSECT

Are you surprised?

So was I until I discovered that a Spider is an Arachnide. The Arachnida family consists of Spiders, Scorpions, and Mites. These beings breathe atmospheric air, have no antennae, and have four pairs of legs attached to the fore parts of the body. The fact that they have more than the normal number of six legs is alone sufficient to separate them from insects.

* * *

ST. PATRICK WAS NOT AN IRISHMAN

THE patron Saint of the emerald isle was a born Frenchman, having first seen the light of day in Tours, France. His real name was Succat. His father's name was Calpurnius, and his mother was a sister of St. Martin, the Bishop of Tours.

BUFFALO BILL NEVER SHOT A BUFFALO IN HIS LIFE

IT IS not my intent to cast aspersions on the famous name of Bill Cody, but it is nevertheless a fact that the valiant old warrior never shot a single buffalo in his long career along the frontiers.

Buffalo Bill was not to blame. He earned his name—but not the name of "Buffalo" Bill, because the only true buffaloes are found in the old world, principally in Africa and India.

The American animal is the bison and is distinctly indigenous to North America.

The bison differs greatly from the buffalo, both in appearance and habits. The buffalo resembles an ox more than a bison, and has short hair besides being very fond of the water.

*   *   *

SEX APPEAL

LADY GOUGH, distinguished blue-nose of England, wrote a book on *Etiquette* in 1863; and on page 80 I find this paragraph:

"The perfect hostess will see to it that the works of male and female authors be properly separated on her bookshelves. Their proximity unless they happen to be married should not be tolerated."

*   *   *

"THE QUEEN OF SPAIN HAS NO LEGS"

WHEN Margaret of Austria, Queen of Philip III, entered Spain in 1599 she passed through a town celebrated for the manufacture of silk stockings; and the authorities, wishing to show her courtesy, presented her with a costly pair. The offer was indignantly refused and the delegates were sternly informed that the "Queen of Spain had no legs."

Since that day of rigid etiquette it has been customary to say that, officially, "the Queen of Spain has no legs."

*   *   *

A PHILADELPHIAN COMMITTED SUICIDE AND LEFT THE FOLLOWING NOTE:

I MARRIED a widow with a grown daughter. My father fell in love with my step-daughter and married her—thus becoming my son-in-law, and my step-daughter became my mother because she was my father's wife.

My wife gave birth to a son, who was, of course, my father's brother-in-law, and also my uncle for he was the brother of my step-mother.

My father's wife became the mother of a son, who was, of course, my brother, and also my grand-child for he was the son of my daughter.

Accordingly, my wife was my grandmother because she was my mother's mother—I was my wife's husband and grandchild at the same time—and, as the husband of a person's grandmother is his grandfather—I AM MY OWN GRANDFATHER!

Mark Twain.

139

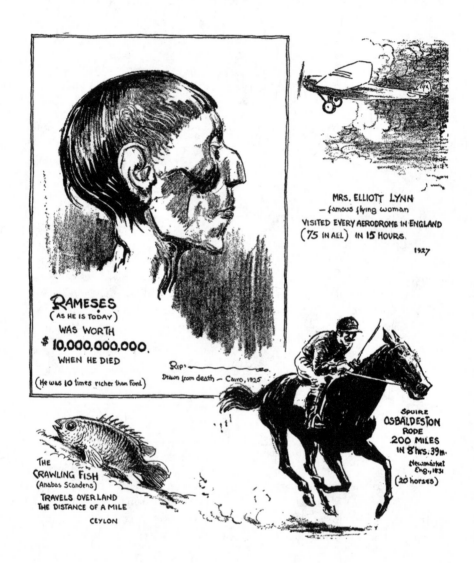

MRS. ELLIOTT LYNN
— famous flying woman
VISITED EVERY AERODROME IN ENGLAND
(75 IN ALL) IN 15 HOURS.
1927

RAMESES
(AS HE IS TODAY)
WAS WORTH
$10,000,000,000.
WHEN HE DIED

(He was 10 times richer than Ford)

Rip'
Drawn from death — Cairo, 1925

SQUIRE
OSBALDESTON
RODE
200 MILES
IN 8 hrs. 39 m.
Newmarket
Eng., 1831
(20 horses)

THE
CRAWLING FISH
(Anabas Scandens)
TRAVELS OVER LAND
THE DISTANCE OF A MILE
CEYLON

THE RICHEST MAN WHO EVER LIVED

RAMESES II, who now serves as a peep-show in the Cairo Museum and as an ad for cigarettes, was once a "ten-billionaire." Ford, Rockefeller, Croesus, and others, were only pikers when compared with the "sunset glory of the royal dynasties of Egypt."

The most famous of the Pharaohs conquered all the kings from Nubia to Syria and exacted great tribute from them. He exploited the gold mines of Nubia for the benefit of his own purse during a period of 67 years. The entire known world of that time contributed to his great wealth and magnificence.

* * *

THE CRAWLING FISH

THIS crawling fish is a native of Asia, and is remarkable for its apparent disregard of certain natural laws. This singular creature has long been noted for its powers of voluntarily leaving the failing streams, ascending the banks, and proceeding over dry land toward some spot where its unerring instinct tells it that water is yet to be found. They sometimes cover a distance of a mile or more, and can live for a period of a week out of water.

On opening the head of the "Anabas Scandens" it will be found that the bones are much enlarged and modified into a series of labyrinthine cells and duplications, so that they retain a large amount of water in the interstices, and prevent the gill-membranes from becoming dry.

* * *

THE HARD RIDING SQUIRE

SQUIRE OSBALDESTON was the most famous sportsman in the world one hundred years ago. The sporting annals of his time are filled with the various events of horsemanship of the doughty old gent. He was of the hard-riding and hard-drinking school of country gentlemen, and when he died he left a legacy of riding records that has never been beaten to this day.

THE TRACER BULLET

Death will find a way.

One day early in February, 1928, A. V. Bonham, of Cotter, Arkansas, saw smoke.

He was startled to learn that it was his own house. It seems that Bonham's little 12-year-old son had used kerosene to start a fire and an explosion followed which set the house in flames.

With the aid of neighbors, Bonham removed most of his household goods. But he overlooked his loaded revolver which reposed in a bureau drawer.

As Bonham stood sadly watching the hungry flames, the report of a pistol rang out. Mack Medley, a neighbor, felt something strike his cap and at the same instant Bonham cried out "I am shot," and clutching his breast, he staggered a few steps and fell dead.

The heat had exploded Bonham's own gun and the bullet had found its mark.

*　*　*

GERMAN INSECT POWER

THERE was a plague of fleas in Münster, Germany in 1670. The High Court of Münster, upon complaint of the burghers, summoned the fleas to appear before it for disorderly conduct. As the fleas disobeyed the summons, they were found guilty, disfranchised and banished for 10 years. The language of the Court decree is very pompous and treats the culprits with withering anger.

*　*　*

"Dear Rip:

Believe it or not? Where do they charge more for a one way ticket than for a round trip? Answer: San Pedro to Los Angeles, Cal., on the Pacific Electric. Men in uniform get special rate of fifty cents round trip and must pay fifty-two cents for a one way ticket.

Heinie Miller."

A REMARKABLE RUNNER

MENSEN ERNST, the Norwegian cross-country runner, was unquestionably the greatest long-distance foot racer that ever lived. The records set up by this tireless Scandinavian in Europe during the early part of the last century have never been equalled. The Indian or Arab has never lived that could keep in sight of him.

Note a few of his records.

Mensen Ernst ran from Paris to Moscow in two weeks. He ran over poor roads, in all kinds of weather, and swam 13 big rivers on the way, yet he averaged 125 miles a day!

He averaged 95 miles a day for 59 days in a race from Constantinople to Calcutta, and return. He swam rivers, crossed deserts, and endured dangers and suffered the blazing sun on his way across Anatolia, Persia, Afghanistan, and India—a distance of 5,625 miles.

Ref.: Life of Mensen Ernst. Pub. by Rieck, Norway.

W.J BRASSARD
~ of Momence, Ill)
HAS ONE BLUE EYE
AND ONE BROWN EYE

JOHN
RADCLIFFE
of GROVE, Pa.

REPORTED FOR WORK
EVERYDAY
INCLUDING SUNDAYS
FOR 26 YEARS

O.T. WERTZ, of Chappell, Neb
CAUGHT THE SAME FISH TWICE !

HE HOOKED A PERCH WHICH BROKE THE LINE AND GOT FREE
6 HOURS LATER HE CAUGHT THE SAME FISH NEARLY A MILE AWAY
July 24, 1926

A BULL FROG
THAT CAUGHT AND ATE MICE
WAS KEPT FOR THAT PURPOSE
BY J. WARD TOMLINSON
Shiloh, Pa., 1915

144

CATCHING THE SAME FISH TWICE

This unusual happening in the gentle art of angling is explained in the affidavit of E. C. Wolf, of Big Springs, Neb., an eyewitness.

"World-Herald,   April 17, 1928.
Omaha, Neb.
Gentlemen:
    July 24, 1926 at 10 A. M., Mr. O. T. Wertz, Chappell, Neb., while fishing in Jumbo Reservoir, which is three miles in diameter, in Colorado, hooked a perch but gut attached to hook broke and fish was lost. The same afternoon this fish was caught by him over half a mile distant from where he hooked it in forenoon, with hook in mouth.

                                        Yours truly,
                                        E. C. Wolf."

* * *

"ONE LONG HOP"

A Chinese baby born in Chicago, Sept. 14, 1927, was so named in honor of Lindbergh.

* * *

Karl Kmetty, a lieutenant in the Hungarian army (1919), convicted of 280 different crimes, sued a Budapest editor for libel.

* * *

As a class, the actors have supplied the largest number of Saints. St. Genest, St. Ardaleon, St. Porphyre, St. Pelagie.

* * *

Heinrich Noste, an Austrian musician, can play tunes on the piano with his tongue.

* * *

Eberhard Wagenes, of London, called his wife a liar 10,000 times for which a statuary fine of $75 was paid.

* * *

Mme. Marie Ollivier, of Hondschoote, Flanders, who committed bigamy, was sentenced to wear two pair of pants around her neck for life.
Ref.: "Registre des sentences criminelles exécutées à Hondschoote sous le règne de Phillippe II."

* * *

The Grand Inquisitor Peter Arbuez, who burned 40,000 people at the stake, was made a Saint by the Pope in 1860.

A QUEEN CROWNED AFTER DEATH

Iñez de Castro, beloved wife of Pedro I of Portugal, became Queen of Portugal after she was dead.

She was assassinated at the instigation of her father-in-law, the King of Portugal, who had other marriage plans for his son. Three years later, when Don Pedro ascended the throne, he had the body of Iñez taken from the grave, placed upon a magnificent throne, arrayed in all the robes of royalty, and crowned "Queen of Portugal" with full ceremony. One fleshless hand held the sceptre and in the other was the orb of royalty while the assembled court did her homage as if she were a living queen.

* * *

Oliver Cromwell was hanged after he was dead.

* * *

The posthumous trial of Pope Formosus is famous. Pope Stephen VII (896-897), for some political reason, had the body of Pope Formosus exhumed and arraigned for trial. A legal defender was appointed and the entire trial was conducted according to the laws of the living. Pope Stephen appeared in person as the prosecutor and won his case, whereupon the body of Formosus was stripped of the papal robes and insignia, mutilated, and thrown into the Tiber.

* * *

The Cid, noted Spanish warrior, led his troops to battle after his death.

In the eleventh book of the "Chronicle of the Cid," Southey relates that the embalmed body of the Spanish warrior was placed in the saddle, according to his wish, and at the head of his army advanced to battle against King Bucar and his countless hosts of Moors . . . winning a great victory.

* * *

Benjamin Franklin invented the harmonica.

* * *

There was never a famous twin.

OLIVER CROMWELL
WAS HANGED
AFTER HE WAS DEAD

TOM M^CAULIFFE
— of Buffalo.
THE ARMLESS GOLFER
PLAYED 18 HOLES
IN 98 STROKES

J. JOHNSON
DROVE THE 'ROYAL SCOT'
300 MILES IN 338 MINUTES WITHOUT
A SINGLE STOP.   1927.
Euston – Carlisle.

147

THE KAISERPOKAL

The most celebrated of all drinks is the drinking of the Kaiserpokal. In fact, it is still celebrated each year with a festival.

In 1616, during the Thirty Years' War, Burgomaster Nusch of Rothenburg on the Tauber saved himself and his city by draining in a single draught the huge stein of seven pints of wine.

Each year the city of Rothenburg commemorates that occasion with a celebration and the present mayor takes a long and ceremonious drink from the same stein—the Kaiserpokal—that Herr Nusch used.

* * *

A COUGH IN THE CAR LOAD

IN 1851, during Napoleon III's coup d'état, when an aide reported that tne mob was facing the Imperial Guard, Count de St. Arnaud, who was just troubled with a cough, exclaimed, "ma sacrée toux!" (my damned cough!). This the aide understood to mean, "massacrez tous" (massacre everybody). The order to fire was given and thousands of human lives were lost.

* * *

HOT DOG

The wonder "weenie" of all time was stuffed by the German Butcher's Guild for their celebration in Koenigsberg in 1601.

This hot dog was more than half a mile long—exactly 3,001 feet—ana required the efforts of 103 butchers to carry it on parade. It weighed 885 pounds and was later equally distributed among the members of the guild at the banquet table.

* * *

FLAMING YOUTH

Charlie Pardie, of Albuquerque, got lit up one night and had a hot time. No wonder.

He drank 15 cans of canned heat in 24 hours.

* * *

"O P Q R S T"

The above letters were sent by Hué in 1867, and were correctly interpreted by the French to read "Au Pecu arresté"—Arrested at Pecu.

* * *

All the books of both the Bible and the Talmud contain no more than 6,654 different words—including derivatives.

GEORGE WASHINGTON WAS *NOT* THE FIRST PRESIDENT OF THE UNITED STATES

THIS is a statement from my daily "Believe It or Not" stint that also caused my readers to doubt—and the mail man to stagger.

Who was the first President—if not Washington?

A man of whom you have never heard—John Hanson, of Maryland.

Although there had been meetings of the Continental Congress from 1774 on, it was not until 1781, when Maryland finally signed the Articles of Confederation, that a union of all the original 13 states became an actuality.

John Hanson, who signed for Maryland, was then elected President of the United States in Congress Assembled, 1781.

George Washington, himself, addressed Hanson as President of the United States in his reply to the latter's message of thanks upon the occasion of the victory of Yorktown.

Ref.: Fiske's "Critical Periods of American History," Senator Dollivar's speech in the Senate, 1910.

* * *

THE HEN THAT BECAME A ROOSTER

THIS apparent impossibility has happened many times. The particular hen chicken that I saw lived, laid eggs, and cackled in its home in a Pennsylvania poultry yard for several years before it manifested anything unusual. Then its owner noticed new sprouting feathers, bright hackles, and the growth of a long drooping tail, and most surprising of all—three full-sized spurs grew on each leg.

The owner, Dr. M. S. Gillespie, brought the bird to the Natural Science Halls of the Brooklyn Museum where the sex-changed chicken was exhibited for some time.

This freak of nature is by no means unprecedented. It is caused by specific changes in the physiological processes—frequently the product of abdominal tuberculosis.

I refer you to Brooklyn Museum Quarterly, October, 1927, and to George P. Engelhardt, Curator, Dept. Natural Sciences, Brooklyn Museum.

SANKAL-WALAH

THE MAN OF CHAINS

THIS Faquir—once a familiar sight in the city of Lahore (India)—was dressed entirely in a mass of heavy chains weighing more than 600 pounds.

He was a Mohammedan. "Sahib Allah Shah" was his name he said, but when you consider the meaning of the words it is obviously an egotistical assertion. The Punjab public called him the "Jingling Faker" and made considerable fuss over him as he slowly crawled along under his self-imposed burden.

"Sankal-Walah"—the "Man of Chains," was an adopted surname, and it became him very well. He began collecting this chain suit of armor when quite a young man—gradually welding on the links and chains, bit by bit, until his groaning load—at the time of his death—weighed 670 pounds.

He had borne this burden for the last 13 years of his life.

* * *

A FLEET CAPTURED BY CAVALRY

THE entire Dutch fleet, ice-bound in the Zuyder Zee, was captured by the French Hussars under Pichegru who galloped across the frozen sea. The Dutch ships were powerful, but, alas—immovable and became easy prey to a charge of cavalry! The result was that the government of the Netherlands collapsed, and Holland was forcibly allied to France (1795).

* * *

"IF YOU WOULD SEE HIS MONUMENT, LOOK AROUND"

The above inscription is placed in St. Paul's Cathedral, London, to the memory of Sir Christopher Wren, who built it.

* * *

MOTHER GOOSE

"Mother Goose" was a real character, and not an imaginary person as has been supposed.

Her maiden name was Elizabeth Foster, and she was born in Boston in 1665. She married Isaac Goose in 1693, and her famous rhymes were written for her grandchildren.

THE GHOST SHIP

THE Gloucester fishing schooner, "Columbia," went to the bottom in a hurricane in August, 1927, with her crew of 20 men. On the following New Year's Day, Capt. Myhre, on the "Ventosta," while dragging the bottom of the sea, caught something with his trawls and suddenly there rose to the surface the battered remains of a dead ship. For a few minutes the "Columbia," with masts erect, remained suspended before the eyes of the startled seamen. Then as suddenly as she had cleft the waves, she disappeared from sight as the 3-inch cables which had hauled her to the surface parted.

* * *

WHAT PRICE PRIVACY

FRANCESCA NORTYUEGE, famous reformer of Dièze, who died in France in 1903, left her fortune to her niece with the proviso that, for the sake of decency, she keep her goldfish always clothed in tights.

* * *

TIP

Comes from the initials of the words "To Insure Promptness."

* * *

HE WHO LAUGHED LAST

Chalchas the Greek died from laughter when the day that was predicted to be his death day came around and the prediction did not seem to materialize.

* * *

A YEAR AND A DAY

A Japanese child is one year old the day it is born.

* * *

Dr. Schmeckegut (taste good) changed his name to Dr. Schmeckebesser (I taste better) in Vienna.

* * *

A case that has been in the Courts since 999. In that year, a wealthy land owner who expected the world to end in 1000, donated the mountain of San Tisone, near Naples, to the Convent of the same name. The world did not perish of course and the owner claimed to cancel his donation. At present the two communities of Ravella and Lettera are still disputing ownership. For 929 years testimony has been taken with never a decision.

THE SHORTEST POEM IN THE WORLD
"Hired.
Tired?
Fired!"

* * *

When I printed the above poem a number of readers called my attention to this one which is even shorter. It is entitled:
"Lines Written on the Antiquity of Microbes"
"Adam
Had 'Em"

* * *

EVEN UP

PATRICK and Eleanor Grady, of Crookhaven (near Cork, Ireland) were born in 1796 in the same house on the same day—were married on the same day—and on the same day fell sick and died on the same day at the ages of 96—leaving 96 descendants.

* * *

IT'S NOT THE HEAT—IT'S THE HUMIDITY!

The thermometer registered 158.8 degrees Fahrenheit in the Oasis of Toauregs, in Northern Africa, 1927.

* * *

THE MORNING AFTER

Herr Reinach, of Vienna, placed a 25-pound cake of ice on his head and allowed it to remain there until it melted. 1928.

* * *

THE JAKUCK WEATHER REPORT

The temperature in Jakuck, Siberia, varied 256.6 degrees in the season of 1928. The thermometer rose from 154.4 below zero to 102.2 degrees above.

* * *

THE FOUNTAIN OF BLOOD

IN THE center of the village of Vertud (Dept. de Gracias) between San Salvador and Guatemala, there is a fountain—"Mina de Sangre"—which ejects a red liquid that coagulates like blood.
"Apuntamientos sobre Centro America," Squier.

* * *

Princess Anthony Kohary, of Hungary, the last of her line, was officially appointed a man. 1889.

FINGER NAILS
OF A CHINESE PRIEST
IN SHANGHAI
22¾ INCHES LONG
He was 27 yrs. growing them

THE FOUR-FOOTED CHICK
Owned by H. G. BOYDEN
ELY, England.

The Pepe-aweto of the Maoris
STRANGEST INSECT ON EARTH —
A CATERPILLAR THAT TURNS
INTO A PLANT.

Is it an insect or a vegetable?

A COMMA THAT SAVED A HUMAN LIFE

MARIA FEODOREWNA accidentally caught sight of the following note appended to the bottom of a death warrant. It was in the handwriting of her husband, Alexander III. It read as follows:

"Pardon impossible, to be sent to Siberia."

Maria transposed the comma so that it read:

"Pardon, impossible to be sent to Siberia." Whereupon the convict was released a free man.

* * *

Professor Netomeff, an Assyriologist, who wrote a book about Nebuchadnezzar, the ancient King of Babylon, was sentenced to perpetual exile in Siberia because the caption of his book, "Nebuchadnezzar," was the same in the Russian language as "Ne boch ad ne tzar" which meant "No God and no Tzar."

* * *

The name of the letter "Q" is the French word "queue"—a tail. In other words, a "Q" is an "O" with a tail.

* * *

Cyrus, King of Persia, knew the name of every soldier in his army by heart.

* * *

Themistocles could call all of the 20,000 inhabitants at Athens by their first names.

* * *

Rev. W. B. Hogg, of El Paso, Texas, memorized the Bible.

* * *

Mrs. Wilhelmine Alff, of Cherokee, Iowa, attended the movies every night for 8 years. 2,927 consecutive evenings.

* * *

Joseph Conrad, famous master of the English language, could not speak a word of it at the age of twenty-five.

* * *

The fiancé of Miss Matilde John, of London, died in 1795. She died 89 years later of a broken heart.

* * *

Señora Salomea Wolf had the portrait of her husband tattooed on her tongue to atone for nagging him to death. Jerez, Spain, 1927.

155

THE editor of The Torch, Central Lake, Mich., assures me that the following paragraph which appeared in his newspaper is nothing but the truth.

"Seven years ago a farmer in Iowa hung his vest on a fence in the barnyard. A calf chewed up a pocket in the garment in which was a gold watch. Last week the animal, a staid old milk cow, was butchered for beef, and the timepiece was found in such a position between the lungs of the cow that respiration—the closing in and filling of the lungs—kept the stemwinder wound up, and the watch had lost but four minutes in the seven years."

* * *

Hastings, Minn.
Dec. 18, 1927.

"My Dear Mr. Ripley:
I have a little item for "Believe It or Not."
A gentleman from my home town by the name of Carl (Tiger) Franklin can swallow three (3) eggs in the shell and cough them up one at a time without breaking the shells.

In my travels into the far corners of the world, this is the only case I ever heard of or seen of this kind. I think this might be mentioned in your "Believe It or Not" section of the papers.
Yours truly,
Wm. Tenner."

* * *

Herman Heidegger, of London, could call from memory the wording of all the signs along both sides of the street for 10 blocks after once walking past to observe them.

* * *

Porson, the Greek scholar, could recite the complete works of Milton—backward and forward.

* * *

La Croze could repeat 12 verses in 12 unknown languages after hearing them read aloud once.

* * *

Arlinin, the Neapolitan, recited 15,350 lines from Dante without a moment's pause.

* * *

Gambetta, the great Tribune, had a wonderful memory. Among other mental feats was his ability to repeat the Book of Ruth word for word backward. He was able to do the same with all the works of Victor Hugo and Ossian.

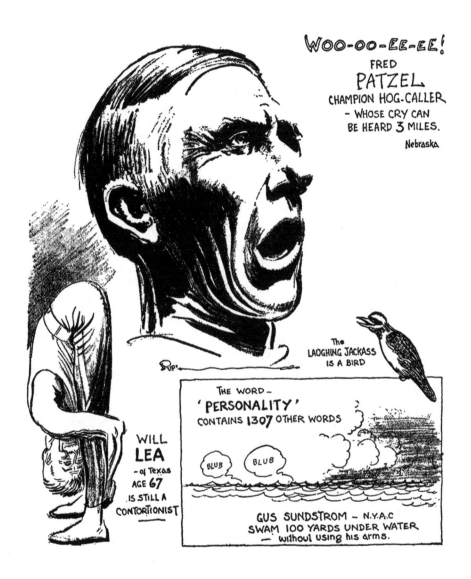

WOO-OO-EE-EE!
FRED PATZEL
CHAMPION HOG-CALLER
— WHOSE CRY CAN
BE HEARD 3 MILES.
Nebraska

The LAUGHING JACKASS IS A BIRD

WILL LEA
— of TEXAS
AGE 67
.IS STILL A
CONTORTIONIST

THE WORD —
'PERSONALITY'
CONTAINS 1307 OTHER WORDS

BLUB   BLUB

GUS SUNDSTROM — N.Y.A.C
SWAM 100 YARDS UNDER WATER
— without using his arms.

THE MENTAL FREAK

DR. CHARLES BERNSTEIN, superintendent of the Rome State School for the Feeble-minded, tells me of a remarkable mental freak who is an inmate of the school at the present time.

"Barney" is 43 years old physically, but his mental age is 6 years. He is unable to read or write, and speaks very indistinctly with a very limited vocabulary, yet he gives instantly the day of the week on which any date falls on either in years past or years to come. Barney never saw a calendar. Several psychologists of note have studied his case but are entirely unable to fathom his mental state."

* * *

THE WILL OF AKBAR THE GREAT

"EVERY man should have four wives; a Hindoo to bear children, a Persian for conversation, an Afghan to keep house, and a Turk to beat up as an example to the others."

* * *

EASY COME EASY GO

SULTAN MURAD IV inherited 240 wives when he assumed the throne of Turkey. He decided to dispense with their help by the simple expedient of putting each wife in a sack and tossing them one by one into the Bosphorus.

* * *

Alexander Richter, placed a wreath on his own grave every week for 60 years. He disappeared, and when he returned he found that the body of a drowned man had been buried as his own under his name.

* * *

Each of the five husbands of Frau Irmgard Bruns, of Berlin, committed suicide. 1928.

* * *

Frank Damek, of Chicago, compiled a complete deck of cards by picking them up from time to time in the street! After 10 years he was 15 cards short. It was another 20 years before he finally completed his deck, in 1890.

THE CRUISE OF THE SKELETONS

"WHILE cruising near the coastline of Punta Arenas (Chile) the British sailing ship 'Johnson' sighted what appeared to be a boat with sails floating in the wind. The British signals eliciting no response, the craft was approached and it was noticed that masts and sails were covered with some kind of green moss, and that the vessel seemed abandoned by its crew. Upon boarding it the skeleton of a man was discovered beneath the helm. The deck was decayed to such an extent that it gave under the footsteps. Three more skeletons were found near a panel, ten were found in the crew's quarters, and six on the bridge. Upon the ravaged prow of the vessel, the words *Marlborough Glasgow* could still be discerned. The Marlborough left Littleton, N. Z. in January 1890, with a cargo of wool and frozen mutton, and a crew of 23 men under command of Captain Hird. It was last seen on its regular course in the Straits of Magellan. In April 1890 an unsuccessful search for the vessel was made. There were also a few passengers on board and one woman."

Reported by the official Agence Havas on Nov. 26, 1913 and by Wellington (New Zealand) Evening Post of Nov. 13, 1913.

* * *

THE MAN WHO DRANK HIMSELF TO DEATH

THE surgeon Dr. Politman, a native of Lorraine, died at the age of 140, having been drunk each day since he was 25 years old. On the eve of his death he performed a major surgical operation successfully.

I refer you Dr. W. Rullman's "Die natürliche Lebensdauer des Menschen" which ran in the "Vossische Zeitung" of Berlin, March 12 and 13, 1916.

* * *

A GOOD LISTENER

WILLIAM MacDONALD, an invalid living in Chula Vista, California, has heard 605 broadcasting stations scattered over the world during the last 3 years. He logged 490 United States stations in every state except South Carolina, and 115 stations outside the country.

THE PENITENT EYE

An eye that misbehaved caused its owner, Herr Heinrich Laufer, to shut it up for ninety days.

It seems that Herr Laufer spied on the wife of his friend and landlord, and then, stricken by his conscience, he confessed his advantage and begged forgiveness. Friend husband was irate and threatened Herr Laufer with a jail sentence for "Ehebruch," but a priest intervened and the matter was amicably settled when the bizarre penance was imposed upon Herr Laufer. The husband kept careful watch over Laufer during the three months.

Ref.: "Duesseldorfer Nachrichten."

* * *

THE LAST NOD OF HOMER

This is the riddle that caused the death of Homer in his vain attempt to solve it—as recorded by Plutarch:

> *"What we caught*
> *We threw away. . .*
> *What we could not catch*
> *We kept."*

Answer: Fleas.

* * *

FARE ENOUGH

SEVERAL years ago Mrs. Frank Scott, of Laporte, Ind., got on a street car with her 13 children and offered the conductor a nickel.

"Pardon, Madame," the conductor said, "but we can't carry a whole Sunday school class for one fare."

"And why not. They are my children and they are all under five years of age," she replied.

Then to settle the argument she produced the family Bible from the luggage and proved to the astounded street car man that none of the thirteen children was over five years of age. Abel and Abner, the youngest, were six months old, and Ashbel, Archer, and Austin, the oldest of the lot, were only four and one-half years of age.

The Laportes had three sets of triplets and two pairs of twins in less than five years!

Fair enough, don't you think so?

* * *

WHAT IS SO RARE AS THIS DAY IN JUNE?

Jan III. Sobieski, King of Poland in the 17th century, was born, crowned, married, and died—each time on the same date of the year—June 17.

HERR
HEINRICH
LAUFER
— of Duesseldorf,

KEPT ONE EYE CLOSED
FOR 90 DAYS

— as a penance for peeping.

JOHN
G.
ANDERSON
HAS WON
600
GOLF
PRIZES

Winged
Foot
Golf Club.

JAY BRUCE
California's official lion hunter
HAS KILLED 284 LIONS

MRS. WM. BURNHAM
of Topsfield, Mass.
OWNS A CAT THAT IS
24
YEARS
OLD

THE SMALLEST CHURCH IN THE WORLD
— Near Latonia, Kentucky — ONLY SEATS 3 PEOPLE

THE LOUDEST NOISE EVER HEARD

THE loudest noise ever heard was on August 27, 1883, when the volcano of Pik Perbuatan, on the Island of Krakatua, exploded in the most violent eruption within historic times, killing 35,147 people. The Island (which lies in the Straits of Sunda between Java and Sumatra) was about three by five miles in size before the eruption but only a small portion now remains.

Four cubic miles of material were blown miles into the air and a dust cloud subsequently spread completely around the world and colored sunsets in distant parts of the globe for three years afterwards. The sound was heard on the Island of Rodriquez, in the Pacific Ocean—3,000 miles away.

* * *

THE EARTH MOVES IN THREE DIFFERENT DIRECTIONS AT THE SAME TIME

1. It rotates upon its own axis with a speed of about 500 yards per second diminishing from the center towards the Poles.

2. It revolves around the sun with a speed of about 19 miles a second.

3. It participates in the sun's own forward motion in the direction of the fixed star, Vega, in the constellation of Lyra, with a speed of 12 miles per second.

All simultaneously.

A fourth movement in which the earth probably participates is that of the sun's own rotation upon its axis which is accomplished once every 25 days.

A fifth movement—that of the whole stellar system upon its axis—is possible—but doubtful.

* * *

"THE HOLY ROMAN EMPIRE" WAS *NOT* HOLY, OR ROMAN, OR AN EMPIRE

It was not holy because it was secular; it was not Roman because it was German; and it was not an empire because its nominal heads—the German kings—ruled in name only.

This Confederation of German States—for that it really was—lasted from Otto I, crowned in 962, to Francis II in 1806.

* * *

PA'S A SAP

The eternal and paternal palindrome. This line reads the same backward as forward. Pa's a sap either way you look at him.

A
LUZONESE
DANCED 172 HOURS
WITHOUT STOPPING

JAPANESE PLUM TREE
500 YEARS OLD IS ONLY 3 FEET HIGH
Osaka

THE BLESSED ISLES

EVERYWHERE in the civilized world except the Channel Islands death and taxes are two absolute certainties of mundane existence. In the islands of Guernsey and Jersey, however, there is much doubt about taxes. King George V cannot impose a single penny per pound on the income of his loyal subjects in these islands unless they waive their ancient privilege.

In fact, no act of Parliament is binding to them until transmitted by order of the King's Privy Council and duly registered there.

* * *

THE BOOZING BISHOP

Johann Fugger, an Italian Bishop, died and willed that—

" . . . A barrel of wine might be annually upset upon his grave so that his body might still sop in that delicious fluid."

He bequeathed a large sum of money to the city of Montefiascone for the maintenance of his purpose.

Ref.: "Central Cities of Italy," by Hare.

* * *

THE ONE-ARMED PAPER HANGER

Yes, there is one. Albert J. Smith, of Dedham, Mass., has but one arm and he is a paper hanger by trade. And he has had the hives too.

* * *

"Bobby" Leach, who went over Niagara Falls in a barrel in 1911, died from injuries received when he slipped on a banana peel while walking quietly along the street in Christchurch, New Zealand, on April 29, 1927.

* * *

THE RIVER THAT RUNS BACKWARDS

The River Tadjoura, on the northeast coast of Africa, flows from the Bay of Tadjoura inland and empties into the Lake of Assal.

* * *

A SQUARE EGG

A chicken owned by James Cook, of New Bedford, Mass. laid a perfectly square egg.

NOMAD
OCANA
MADAM
ANACO
DAMON

AN AMERICAN
PALINDROME
—by Doc Applegate
Ogallala, Neb.

THERE IS A
NEWSPAPER
PUBLISHED FOR
BEGGARS
IN PARIS

HIROHITO
of JAPAN

IS THE 124th EMPEROR
OF THE SAME FAMILY !

THE JAPANESE ROYAL FAMILY IS THE OLDEST
FAMILY IN THE WORLD — AND HAS
MAINTAINED AN UNBROKEN LINE FROM —
JIMMU TENNO —2588 YRS. AGO

WALTER
HAGEN
PLAYED 18 HOLES
IN 59 STROKES
Zurich
May 23, 1928

165

THE WORLD'S WORST THUG

B UHRAM, who gleefully murdered 931 men, was a member of the Thuggee sect—a gang of professional murderers who flourished in India in 1830 before the English suppressed them. The Thugs were worshippers of Bhowanee; and to this god they sacrificed anybody that came handy; but they were careful to keep the dead man's things themselves as they believed the god cared only for the corpse. Men were initiated into this sect with solemn ceremonies. Then they were taught how to strangle a person with the sacred choke-cloth, but were not allowed to perform officially with it until after long practice. It required practice to choke a man expertly. Then the job was done instantaneously; the cloth was whipped around the victim's neck, there was a sudden twist, and the head fell silently forward, the eyes starting from the sockets; and all was over.

Mark Twain tells of Thuggee in "Following the Equator."

*   *   *

Robert (Lefty) Grove, the star pitcher of Connie Mack's Athletics is generally considered to be the best pitcher in baseball today. He has tremendous speed and a great curve which has always caused his opponents to swing aimlessly.

He recently struck out 5 men with 16 pitched balls: there were no fouls.

The record depicted opposite was made while he was a member of the Baltimore club, about 5 years ago.

*   *   *

HEAVEN ONLY KNOWS!

A letter addressed to "GOD" was forwarded to Rome from Liptau, Germany, in 1926. It was returned to the sender marked "Addressee Unknown."

*   *   *

SOLVING THE SERVANT PROBLEM

C OUNTESS ELIZABETH BATHORY, the famous Hungarian "tigress" (1560-1614), killed 650 servant girls in 6 years. Being a noble woman she was immune from punishment.

THE WORLD'S WORST THUG
BUHRAM — MURDERED **931** MEN IN **40** YEARS !

Rip — Drawn in INDIA

LEFTY GROVES
of Baltimore
STRUCK OUT **68** MEN
IN **45** INNINGS
1923

Miss
LUCILLE NOONAN
San Francisco telephone operator
HAS MEMORIZED 2000 NUMBERS

A TOAD HOPPED 75 MILES IN 5 DAYS
from Wakefield to Old Center, Mass. June, 1923
OWNED BY FREDERICK SIDNEY.

167

THE MAN WITH THE GOLDEN NOSE

TYCHO BRAHE, the Danish astronomer, lost his nose in a duel with Passberg and adopted a golden one, which he attached to his face by a cement which he carried about with him. That nose is distinctly discernible in all of his portraits.

I refer you to Marryat: Jutland and the Danish Isles p. 305 ("that eminent man who had a golden nose, Tycho Brahe").

* * *

AN EMPRESS'S AGILE EARS

THE Empress Marie Louise's ability to move her ears at will and to turn them inside out, is reported in the Mémoires of M. H. d'Alméras, Chamberlain to the French Court. Madame la Duchesse d'Abrantès, one of the Empress's ladies-in-waiting, also wrote of it.

They add that this was one of the great distractions at the Court of Napoleon III, and that the Emperor himself would hasten to the Salon whenever the Empress could be induced to perform.

* * *

FRIDAY UNLUCKY?

Friday is the luckiest day in American history.

Friday, Aug.　3, 1492—Columbus sailed for America.
Friday, Oct. 12, 1492—Columbus discovered America.
Friday, Nov. 22, 1493—Columbus landed here again.
Friday, June 12, 1494—Mainland of South America discovered.
Friday, Mar.　5, 1496—Henry VIII. commissioned Cabot which resulted in the discovery of North America.
Friday, Sept.　7, 1565—Mendez founded St. Augustine, Florida, the oldest city in the U. S.
Friday, Nov. 10, 1620—Pilgrim Fathers landed in harbor of Provincetown.
Friday, Feb. 22, 1732—George Washington born.
Friday, Oct. 17, 1777—Burgoyne surrendered at Saratoga.
Friday, Sept. 19, 1781—Cornwallis surrendered at Yorktown.

* * *

Shakespeare's daughter could not read or write.

* * *

Madame de Maintenon, morganatic wife of Louis XIV., had herself bled regularly twice a week, in order not to blush at the stories told at Court.

TOM WEDDERS, of Yorkshire, HAD A NOSE 7½ IN LONG

400 WORDS IN ENGLISH BEGINNING WITH "SN". APPLY TO THE NOSE — and its activities —

SNOUT
SNIFF
SNEEZE
SNORE
SNICKER
SNEER
SNUB
SNOOT
SNO
SNI
SN
S

The Empress MARIE LOUISE COULD FOLD HER EARS AT WILL — AND ALSO TURN THEM INSIDE OUT !

A TELEGRAM WAS SENT AROUND THE WORLD IN 8 MINUTES. 1927

TERRY McGOVERN WON THE BANTAM AND FEATHERWEIGHT CHAMPIONSHIPS AND KNOCKED OUT THE LIGHTWEIGHT CHAMPION — AND WAS THROUGH AT 21.

ONE PAIR OF SHOES FOR BOTH! FATHER AND SON ARE BOTH NAMED ALBERT FARLER — BOTH LOST A LEG AND BOTH WEAR THE SAME SIZE SHOE.

Kildonan, Man., Canada

169

FIRE WATER

It actually happened.

Fables about breath catching fire became a fact in Lodz, Russia.

After drinking a quantity of vodka, a workman named Stobb tried to blow out a match with which he was lighting a cigarette with fatal result.

Flames shot from his mouth and an explosion followed, Stobb falling to the floor unconscious and dying shortly afterward.

* * *

"My Dear Mr. Ripley:

Here is a little article good for your column. There is a fellow I know whose first name starts with "A" and his last with "Z." His name is Alfred Zimbalist, and he lives on "A" Ave., St. John., Apt. "A" A 31, and his phone number extension is A31.

He eats Apples and Asparagus every day, and loves the smell of Zinc. It's very peculiar but, believe it or not, that's the truth.

Respectfully,

Sydney Retchetk,
321 W. 44th St., New York."

* * *

THE CHEESE CHAMPION

Zoroaster, the famous Persian lawgiver and founder of the religion of the Parsees, lived on nothing but cheese for thirty years.

* * *

WHOOPEE

THE Mayor of Grand Lemps, France, issued an ordinance that any inhabitant may enter a saloon and drink his fill and then leave without paying. He was a prohibitionist.

Ref.: "Bibliothèque Historique," 1818, vol. 1, page 317.

* * *

A RECORD TO BE SNEEZED AT

James Lanvier, of Edinburgh, sneezed 690 times in succession. 1927.

THE FIJI FIRE-WALKERS

"VILAVILAIREVO," the annual fire-walking ceremony of the Fiji-Islanders during which the natives walk and dance with bare feet on white-hot rocks without burning themselves, has long puzzled travelers. Apparently the Fijians are immune to pain. They walk nimbly over the glowing rocks without so much as a blister.

First, a circular shallow pit about thirty feet across is dug and filled with dry branches and fire wood. A torch is applied and then the stones are rolled in on the blazing pit and allowed to heat for half a day. Green leaves are next scattered over the white-hot stones causing clouds of steam to rise in dramatic fashion and the dance of the fire-walkers begins.

Ah—there are tricks to all trades; even fire-walking! I have the Fijian secret. Sh-h-h! The stones are of volcanic origin and so porous that they do not retain the heat although they appear to be white-hot; and the heavy green leaves protect the feet of the dancers.

*　*　*

THE $4,412,000-A-YEAR-MAN

THE largest salary every received by any one man was that drawn down by the late Franz Josef I, Emperor of Austria. It amounted to $4,412,000 or 22,060,000 Kronen annually. This was strictly a salary and must not be confused with his income from other sources.

During his lifetime, Franz Josef drew $274,600,000 from the Austrian state. This amounts to more than 25 times the total salary of all the Presidents of the United States combined.

*　*　*

THE $2,000,000 COMMA

A clerk in Congress, instead of writing
"All foreign fruit-plants are free from duty,"
wrote
"All foreign fruit, plants are free from duty."
It was impossible to change this mistake until a new session of Congress met.

*　*　*

MAMMY!

ON December 2, 1927, little Marie Finster jumped from the roof of a building in Vienna and was saved from death by falling into the arms of her mother who happened to be passing along the street below at that very minute.　　　　　　　　　　　　　　　　　　—*Vienna Tageblatt.*

*　*　*

THE LAST WILL OF RABELAIS

"I have nothing. I owe much. The rest I leave to the poor."

172